Social Capital

Key Concepts Series

Social Capital

Joonmo Son

polity

First published in 2020 by Polity Press

Polity Press
65 Bridge Street
Cambridge CB2 1UR, UK

Polity Press
101 Station Landing
Suite 300
Medford, MA 02155, USA

ISBN-13: 978-1-5095-1378-9
ISBN-13: 978-1-5095-1379-6(pb)

A catalogue record for this book is available from the British Library.

Library of Congress Cataloging-in-Publication Data

Names: Son, Joonmo, author.
Title: Social capital / Joonmo Son.
Description: Medford : Polity, 2020. | Series: Key concepts | Includes bibliographical references and index. | Summary: "Much-needed critical assessment of a ubiquitous concept in the social sciences"-- Provided by publisher.
Identifiers: LCCN 2019050898 (print) | LCCN 2019050899 (ebook) | ISBN 9781509513789 (hardback) | ISBN 9781509513796 (paperback) | ISBN 9781509513826 (epub)
Subjects: LCSH: Social capital (Sociology)
Classification: LCC HM708 .S666 2020 (print) | LCC HM708 (ebook) | DDC 302--dc23
LC record available at https://lccn.loc.gov/2019050898
LC ebook record available at https://lccn.loc.gov/2019050899

Typeset in 10.5 on 12pt Sabon
by Fakenham Prepress Solutions, Fakenham, Norfolk NR21 8NL
Printed and bound in Great Britain by CPI Group (UK) Ltd, Croydon

For further information on Polity, visit our website:
politybooks.com

Mi-Kyeong, Hahae, and Hajin,
the structural basis of social capital to which I belong

Contents

Preface

Social capital is without doubt a principal concept in social sciences. It is rare that a concept is adopted by multiple disciplines, forms its independent area of studies within them, impacts public policies, and receives great media exposure. Social capital has been the exception. In short, it is popular. However, this popularity has taken its toll. Social capital suffers from a lack of consensus in terms of its meaning and measurement because various researchers and disciplines developed their own ways of utilizing the concept. Thus I cannot pretend that there is a common definition.

The practical way in which I choose to introduce social capital in this book is (1) by showing diverse theoretical approaches proposed by key scholars analyzing their commonalities and differences, and (2) by discussing what kind of impact social capital has made in various research areas. In doing so, I apply an analytical typology comparing individual and collective social capitals to main theoretical approaches and, using the same typology, organize the contributions that social capital has made to various research areas. Briefly, individual social capital refers to shared resources among the members of a personal network, while collective social capital indicates common consciousness, relational features, and pooled assets of a collectivity such as a neighborhood, a voluntary association, or a whole society. However, I use this typology not because it is ideal but because it is a practical means to produce a systematic review of the unorganized social capital literature.

To make a significant improvement, I suggest that the concept of social capital should be delimited. The three-step approach from preconditions to structural basis to production of social capital aims to delimit the concept separating cultural-psychological-institutional-legal factors from it. According to this approach, for instance, collective social capital should be composed of the group-level and individual assets attached to organizational networks, taking collective consciousness (e.g., trust) and relational features (e.g., norms of reciprocity) back to be part of the preconditions of the structural basis of social relations, not social capital per se.

I can suggest two strategic ways of reading this book. Readers interested in the theories and measurements of social capital may first read chapters 1, 2, and 7. Those who want to know how social capital is applied to certain areas of their interest can go to chapters 3 to 6.

I would like to thank Nan Lin, John Wilson, and Edward A. Tiryakian for their intellectual influences on me that are reflected in this book. Vineeta Sinha, my department head, allowed me to take a sabbatical semester to complete this book. Gabriel Noparat, my research assistant, has done a great job in helping me review numerous studies of social capital in various fields. Cyndy Brown has copy-edited the manuscript meticulously. I am grateful to Jonathan Skerrett, Karina Jákupsdóttir, Evie Deavall, and the copy-editors at Polity, who have offered valuable advice as well as assistance with the publication of this book.

Acknowledgment

This work was supported by the NUS Global Asia Institute-JY Pillay Comparative Asia Research Center grant [CARC-2016-001].

1
What is Social Capital?

Social capital has become a popular concept across the globe in the past few decades. Governments, international organizations, nonprofit organizations, multinational corporations, educational institutions, religious entities, and old and new media use the term frequently for various issues as if it can solve, or at least help resolve, grim social, political, economic, or communal ills. However, it is definitely wrong to assume that social capital has always meant something uniform or coherent. Rather, the term has all too often held diverse meanings, depending on who uses it for what purpose. Thus it is not surprising that Wikipedia remarks, "Social capital has multiple definitions, interpretations, and uses." Considering that the definition of social capital that appeared in the same Wikipedia page (https://en.wikipedia.org/wiki/Social_capital) vividly exemplifies the status quo of the concept, let us mull over for a moment the very sentence in which the open-access web encyclopedia manifested the term's tremendous multiplicity: "Social capital is a form of economic and cultural capital in which social networks are central, transactions are marked by reciprocity, trust, and cooperation, and market agents produce goods and services not mainly for themselves, but for a common good."

Frankly, I do not understand this definition, although I appreciate the endeavor to provide it, whoever did so. Most of all, the problem is that it is unclear what social capital actually is, even after intently studying this sentence several times, word by word, phrase by phrase. Specifically, if social capital is "a form of economic and cultural capital," how then does it differentiate itself from the other two types of capitals? What does it mean by "social networks are *central* in social capital"? Does this centrality imply that social networks themselves are social capital or that, as infra-structure, they keep social capital together? The definition also goes further, maintaining that transactions within social capital show features of "reciprocity, trust, and cooperation." More questions arise. First, are these transactions economic in their nature? Then why, all of a sudden, do such transac-tions appear in the definition without any prior clue? Second, are reciprocity, trust, and cooperation confined to those transactions per se, or do they in reality indicate general characteristics of social capital? This question comes up because a few renowned scholars have proposed that social capital is made up of trust and norms of reciprocity separate from or, rather, aligned with social networks (Coleman 1990; Putnam 2000). Then, the last part of the definition claims that in social capital "market agents produce goods and services" mainly for a common good. Is it realistic to claim that actors in markets furnish goods and services for community at the expense of their self-interest? Is this not too naive a thought? With regard to these queries, I can provide neither definite answers nor convincing clues to get at them. Just before the publication of this book, I have found that the Wikipedia page does not any longer present the problematic definition. Instead, it now lists multiple definitions of social capital made by several theorists.

Further, it is not only the formal academic discussions of social capital but also the ways in which mass media introduced the concept to the general public that have from time to time shown such a whole host of problems akin to those mentioned. For instance, the weekly *New York Times Magazine* ran feature stories for the first half of the year 2016 about celebrities who frequently used social media such as Instagram or Twitter. Interestingly, the magazine put those articles under the series title of "Social Capital" (https://www.nytimes.com/column/social-capital). The first feature story highlighted Cher, an established American singer and actress, who had 2.7 million followers on Twitter. The focal concern of the story was that, although she habitually made careless mistakes in grammar, spelling, or spacing in her Twitter messages and, moreover, often posted about very personal matters, she was still well received by her followers. At the end of the day, one may wonder how such stories are relevant to social capital. Nonetheless, each of the series articles began with an introductory statement: "Welcome to Social Capital, a series devoted to analyzing the social media presences of celebrities." Thus it seems that the weekly magazine editor(s) and staff writers thought that celebrities' social media exposure to the public can somehow be called social capital. Those bidirectional electronic media as a whole may have enabled a brand new way of communication between entertainers and their fans, unheard of or unseen before the internet era; still, it is a quite different issue if this sort of new phenomenon arising from popular two-way social media is social capital. This unrestrained usage of the term "social capital" in various old and new media stems from how it has been ambiguously formed and developed in the academia, as noted by Durlauf and Fafchamps (2004: 62): "the extravagant claims often found in this literature ... capable of attributing every conceivable societal virtue to social capital." And as was rightly pointed out in the mid-1990s, "the more social capital is celebrated for a growing list of wonderful effects, the less it has any distinct meaning" (Portes and Landolt 1996: 18).

Then what is social capital? It is one thing to criticize rampant and, not infrequently, capricious usage of a concept but quite another to clarify what it really means. Moreover, it is an onerous job to draw the conceptual boundary elucidating what social capital is and thus, naturally, what it actually is not. This sounds an almost impossible task, considering diverse approaches to social capital by various social science disciplines and their subareas; who would like it if somebody said, "Your conceptualization of social capital is irrelevant"? Obviously, nobody is entitled to claim a monopoly over social capital. Hence this issue can potentially stir up an obnoxious pseudo-political turmoil – or invoke an insidious ignorance of such claims – among scholars and practitioners involved in social capital.

All things considered, it is not the main aim of this book to develop a battlefield for a theoretical war. Instead, its principal purpose is a general introduction to the concept, theory, and practical applications and limitations of social capital. And, as will be shown soon, the following chapters are structured pretty much in that order. This also fits the goals of Polity's Key Concepts series. Nevertheless, numerous books have introduced social capital in different ways (e.g., Baron, Field, and Schuller 2000; Bartkus and Davis 2009; Dasgupta and Serageldin 2000; Field 2008; Halpern 2005). Thus yet another general introduction would be redundant. To ensure this monograph is a meaningful contribution to the debate, I therefore propose a bidimensional categorization of social capital: namely, *collective* social capital and *individual* social capital. Detailed explications of them follow. In later chapters, major substantive applications of the concept appear in accordance with this categorization. It is necessary to take an eclectic position acknowledging these two representative approaches so that unwanted confusions and contestations may be defused and, more importantly, so future studies may adopt this conceptual categorization and position their contributions accordingly.

However, this dimensional ideation of social capital is not new. For instance, some scholars made similar distinctions between bonding and bridging social capital (Putnam 2000: 22–3, 2007), public and private social capital (Leana and van Buren 1999), communal and linking social capital (Oh, Kilduff, and Brass 1999 [cited in Adler and Kwon 2002]), relational and system social capital (Esser 2008), or participation and trust social capital (van Beuningen and Schmeets 2013) for various reasons such as conceptual refinement or improving empirical measurement. More specifically, the differentiation between collective and individual social capital has also appeared in the literature. Yet it is rare that these two are discussed as a complementary pair. This is mainly because the authors want to highlight either the collective (e.g., Newton 2001) or the interpersonal (e.g., Van der Gaag and Snijders 2004) nature of social capital at the expense of the other. In a sense, collective and individual social capital, though seemingly coupled, indicate rather how the literature has been deeply divided along these lines. Nevertheless, I find it helpful to reorganize the social capital literature employing the categorization. By doing so, I aim to build a bridge between these two distinct theoretical approaches. After all, collective and individual social capital concepts may not be as disparate as they seem, although differences exist between them. In the remainder of this chapter, I describe social capital theories in general by summarizing contributions of several key scholars and then, against this backdrop, provide a distinctive categorization of collective and individual social capital.

Various social capitals

To gain a deeper understanding of what it is, we first need to be aware of how the very idea of social capital came into being. There are key scholars who have offered crucial insights. Specifically, Marx, Coleman, Bourdieu, Putnam, Fukuyama, and Lin have made remarkable contributions to the literature.

Marxist macroeconomic view of social capital

It should be helpful to see how Karl Marx, one of the founding fathers of sociology and the inventor of the concept of capital, understood and used the term "social capital." Reviewing Marx's contribution shows again what diverse meanings social capital has, including his literal interpretation of this two-word phrase.

For Marx, social capital – *gesellschaftlichen Kapitals* in the original German text – is simply the sum total of individual capitals in a country:

> The many individual capitals invested in a particular branch of production have compositions which differ from each other to a greater or lesser extent. The average of their individual compositions gives us the composition of the total capital in the branch of production under consideration. Finally, the average of all the average compositions in all branches of

production gives us the composition of the total social capital of a country ... (Marx 1990 [1867]: 762–3)

This point becomes more obvious when he depicts the relationship between individual capitals and social capital in the process of capital accumulation and concentration:

> Every individual capital is a larger or smaller concentration of means of production, with a corresponding command over a larger or smaller army of workers ... The growth of the social capital is accomplished through the growth of many individual capitals. All other circumstances remaining the same, the individual capitals grow, and with their growth the concentration of the means of production increases, in the proportion in which they form aliquot parts of the total social capital. (Marx 1990 [1867]: 776)

As stated, social capital for Marx is the aggregated total volume of individual capitals, and thus it is possible in principle that social capital can be divided and attributed to individual capitalists. So considering that social capital is an aggregate of all the material resources spread across a society, Marx sometimes uses social wealth, another term, interchangeably with social capital. Thus it sounds almost as if social capital arises naturally out of the collaborative capitalist production system to the extent that it can be equated with the total amount of wealth in a society. This is far from so. On the contrary, he stresses that individual capitalists are in strong competition as commodity producers, and therefore, for instance, the centralization or huge growth of capital in one place presumes massive losses in another. Hence social capital can only exist hypothetically because it is impossible to pool all individual capitals in a capitalist system where cut-throat competition prevails. If we go a step further, we may conclude that social capital can eventually be realized only when a capitalist country goes through a revolutionary change to socialism in which a centralization of material resources is licitly executed by the polity.

Two more critical points need to be discussed in regard to the Marxist ideation of social capital. First, Marx did not even suggest that a *network* of individual capitalists is a prerequisite for creating social capital. Again, social capital

Table 1.1 Typology of individual or collective social capital

THEORIST: Typology and components	Marx	Coleman	Bourdieu	Putnam	Fukuyama	Lin
Individual or collective social capital	Collective (hypothetical existence)	Both collective and individual	Collective	Both collective and individual	Collective	Individual
Key definition of social capital	Aggregated total volume of individual capitals	Multiple functional entities composed of both structural features and individual actions	Aggregate of resources in a durable network of ruling class	Tripartite entity of social networks, norms of reciprocity, trustworthiness	Instantiated informal norm that promotes cooperation, capability that arises from the prevalence of trust	Resources embedded in a social structure
Agency	Capitalists	Individuals in closed communities, communal organizations	Ruling class	Individuals in networks and communities, voluntary associations, nation-states	Nation-states in principle (aggregated responses from individuals in actual analyses)	Individuals in networks
Measurement of agency	Means of production and material resources owned by individual capitalists	Actors within network, exchange of credits and obligations	Institutionalized network ties of mutual acquaintance and recognition	Number of membership in voluntary associations, generalized trust	Generalized trust, radius of trust, level of trust	Network features and resources
Projected objectives	Accumulation of social (national) wealth	Public goods, private gains	Maintenance and transfer of class positions and fungible assets	Mostly public and sometimes private goods	Reduction of transaction costs, increase in collective goods	Instrumental and expressive private gains
Measurement of objectives	Amount of virtual social (national) wealth	Educational outcomes, communal bonding, civic engagement	Fungible assets (i.e., economic, cultural, human capitals)	Economic development, democracy, or civil society	Liberal democracy, marketization	Status attainment, well-being
Major level of analysis	Nation-state	Individual, community	Class	Individual, community, nation-state	Nation-state	Individual

for him is neither more nor less than a virtual sum total of individual capitals. Therefore Marx did not have to render details of how to create, maintain, or dissolve it. Had he done so, he should then have proposed a specific way to build a collectively owned capital that, like it or not, would naturally require networks or certain forms of collaborative connections among individual capitalists, whatever we call them. In short, social capital for Marx exists without networks, not to mention other widely known features such as trust or norms of reciprocity. Second, laborers do not have any stake in social capital because they do not own capital in the first place. Thus laborers, the absolute majority in any nation, are excluded from the Marxist conception of social capital. With regard to this complete exclusion of laborers, Farr (2004) points out that using the concept of social capital, Marx wanted to underline that although social capital, the total wealth of a nation, is solely a product of labor, ironically it is possessed by only a small fraction of capitalists. Some critical features of Marx's social capital are summarized in Table 1.1, along with those of five other theorists.

Micro foundation of social capital

In stark contrast to this macroeconomic deterministic view of Marx, the current social capital literature has blossomed with studies of intimate interactions in small groups, initiated originally by Georg Simmel (1955 [1922]). Indisputable is the fact that social ties, the building blocks of social capital, develop from the smallest possible interactions in family or friendship. Detailing daily ordinary interactions in an Irish farm family as an example, George C. Homans (1951) maintains that a conceptual scheme of social sciences is composed of persons and three elements of their behavior: activity, interaction, and sentiment. Specifically, dyadic (that is, comprising two individuals) or triadic (comprising three) relations in a group may involve certain sentiments – either friendly or antagonistic – that in turn promote activities between or among themselves. As we will see below, the sentiments that Homans introduces may include trust and trustworthiness as well, highly relevant concepts to social capital according to Putnam (2000) and Fukuyama (1995a). For instance, Fukuyama describes trust as a "proclivity of spontaneous sociability" (1995a: 29), which is akin to Homans's friendly sentiment. At any rate, pursuing such formed activities through interactions, people weave a web that can hold social resources or debts. And these smallest possible units of human groupings, when accumulated, can eventually be expanded to a large-scale social system. As to the purpose and contents of activities (or behaviors), Homans (1958) proposes that it is mainly for exchange. In particular, Homans claims, "social behavior is an exchange of goods, material goods but also non-material ones, such as symbols of approval or prestige" (1958: 606). Persons in exchange relations with others exert efforts to increase rewards and reduce costs so as to increase profit margins (Profit = Reward − Cost). Hence this exchange theory of social behavior is closely associated with economics and, more specifically, rational choice perspective.

In one way or another, subsequent theorists were affected by this baseline view of social relations in small groups, as a result of which most of them acknowledge the micro-foundation of social capital.

Coleman: social capital as macro structure and micro actions

A representative scholar is James S. Coleman whose major contribution was to the sociology of education, particularly with regard to the educational achievement of adolescents (Coleman 1961). Bringing us closer to the current literature of social capital, Coleman (1988, 1990) coins the idea of social capital on the basis of personal interactions in closed communities. He found that social capital is instrumental in reducing dropout rate of high-school students. As one of his articles, entitled "Social Capital in the Creation of Human Capital," suggests, he highlights the virtues of social capital because it helps teenagers complete high-school education, thanks in particular to the mutual credit and obligation exchanged between parents in the community to protect and guide their schoolchildren. He specifically proposes several forms of social capital that include mutual credit and obligation (Coleman 1990: 304–13). For instance, social capital takes the form of obligations and expectations among actors who exchange various forms of assistance. Situated in long-term relationships within a communal boundary, when one person gets a helping hand from someone else, he or she is obligated to return the favor if asked in the future. Thus Coleman describes that accepting help is like issuing a credit slip. This reciprocal giving and receiving grows among members of a community. And when such social exchanges are consistently conducted among a majority of communal members for a long time, people establish social capital. Additionally, social capital thus created can also act as an information channel between those engaged in reciprocal social exchange. That is, when a person in the community learns new information, it can spread through the pre-established communal network.

Interestingly, Coleman goes beyond the interpersonal actions of exchange and suggests other collective forms of social capital, such as norms and effective sanctions, authority relations, intentional organization, and appropriable social organization. Specifically, norms and sanctions are a necessary condition for initiating and promoting social exchange among actors in a community. When one betrays a norm – for instance, neglecting to pay back a favor – set up in a community, one exposes oneself to communal sanctions. In this way, social capital can be viewed as a public good growing out of private goods. Next, authority relations articulate that members of a community agree to delegate their rights of control to a certain person so that the selected leader can be in charge of expanding social capital on behalf of others. This describes in some sense how a representative democracy emerges from grassroots interpersonal relations. Then intentional organization indicates that collectivities of various kinds, based upon and independently from interpersonal relations, come into being with purposive aims. In short, organizations are collectivized social capital that purposively aims to fulfill a predefined set of goals. Nonetheless, organizations tend to work for some other goals that were neither originally planned nor intended. This phenomenon is called appropriable social organization. For instance, it is common to see that Facebook, a virtual social network service for friends near and far, also functions as a news feed for political campaigns, a conduit for job referrals, or a recruitment channel for various volunteering opportunities.

Therefore, Coleman conceptualizes social capital as public good, although he began his discussion from micro-social relations. Specifically, his basic idea of social capital is depicted in a simple figure of a three-person structure, where three dots form a triangle connected by three lines (Coleman 1990: 305, Figure 12.1). He then describes the three dots as human capital and the lines connecting the dots as the social capital existing in mutual relations. He also concentrates on familial relations. In particular, he breaks down family background (socioeconomic status) into financial, human, and social capitals (Coleman 1988: S109–S110). Then he argues that the presence of each type of capital can help grow other types. For example, he describes how John Stuart Mill greatly benefited from his father, James Mill, who taught his son Latin and Greek prior to school age and also encouraged John to intellectually engage with Jeremy Bentham, the founder of utilitarianism. This extraordinary case indicates how familial social ties can affect the human capital growth of the next generation. Of course, then, there are the connections between like-minded families in a community that exchange favors. He calls such communal relations social capital, outside the family. In this way, social capital grows from private good to public good. Thus it is not surprising that Coleman stresses both individual actions and social structure in his definition of social capital:

> Social capital is defined by its function. It is not a single entity, but a variety of different entities having two characteristics in common: They all consist of some aspect of a social structure, and they facilitate certain actions of individuals who are within the structure ... Unlike other forms of capital, social capital inheres in the structure of relations between persons and among persons. (Coleman 1990: 302)

Therefore, Coleman's social capital is flexible enough to cover interpersonal relations as well as communal and organizational entities. Further, although he acknowledges that a certain form of social capital can be valuable for some but harmful to others, in general his social capital begets positive externalities for both individuals and collectivities. In short, the wide scope of the concept and its functionalist features constitute both the merits and the controversies of Coleman's contribution. On the one hand, they have helped make social capital widely known and attractive to various academic disciplines and practitioners; and yet they have, on the other hand, enabled untethered applications of the concept to numerous agenda at all conceivable levels – individual, organizational, national, or international. Interestingly, Coleman is commonly acknowledged as a seminal theorist of social capital by Putnam (2000: 19–20, 302–3), Fukuyama (1995a: 10, 2001: 8), and Lin (2001: 22–8), whose theoretical approaches are distinct from one another.

Bourdieu: social capital of the ruling class

Pierre Bourdieu, the inventor of cultural capital theory, is one of the most widely cited scholars in the social capital literature, although he did not write much about it. He argues that, apart from possession of economic capital, the ruling class has pathways to maintain and transfer its class position and resources to future generations. For example, with respect to cultural capital, a taste for high-class culture (e.g., classical music, arts) is hard to acquire if lacking the appropriate familial support for systematic private tutoring – including within-family teaching – and formal education through childhood (Bourdieu 1984). Likewise, an invisible but solid network among members of the ruling class is another way in which it shares multiple resources within the class boundary and thus keeps other classes at bay. This idea clearly surfaces in Bourdieu's definition of social capital (1980: 2, 1986: 248): "Social capital is the aggregate of the actual or potential resources which are linked to possession of a durable network of more or less institutionalized relationships of mutual acquaintance or recognition." As shown in the definition, a representative feature of Bourdieu's theory is that social capital is perceived as the pooled resources attached to a group network, particularly that of the ruling class. In short, his social capital is capital co-owned and shared within the ruling class. This view is similar to Marx's in that Marxist social capital is the aggregated total volume of individual capitals. And yet a critical difference is that Bourdieu argues that a network of mutual acquaintance helps integrate and reproduce the ruling class's resources generation after generation, whereas Marx does not propose any connective mechanism that may link material resources owned by individual capitalists.

Apart from functioning as a pathway to retain and transfer class positions, Bourdieu's social capital exhibits a few more crucial features. That is, while acknowledging that social capital cannot be fully independent of other forms of capital, he also suggests that it engenders a multiplier effect in addition to preexisting capitals (Bourdieu 1986: 249). This means that social capital can create greater value than economic, human, and cultural capitals have already produced. Further, social capital as a form of capital can be converted to economic capital when the necessary conditions are met. This is why Portes (2000: 2) underlines, "Bourdieu's key insight was that forms of capital are fungible." This fungibility, or convertibility, among capitals renders social capital a quantifiable asset, a distinct theoretical divergence, for instance, from Putnam and Fukuyama. In contrast, those who object to the idea of social "capital" stress that it is far from being materialized as a calculable entity. Specifically, they ask how trust, social relations, numbers of associations or membership in them, norms of reciprocity, or sociability can be quantified in the way that one is able to count the exact dollar amounts of annual salaries, housing prices, utility bills, or train fares. Fischer (2005) refutes the idea that social capital is fungible by bluntly asking Putnam, in his book review of *Bowling Alone*, "What's the Score?" He then goes on to criticize the concept of social capital almost derisively: "It is a metaphor that misleads: Where can I borrow social capital? What is the going interest rate? Can I move some of my social capital off-shore?" (Fischer 2005: 157). I do not think that any theorist, including Marx, can calculate its interest rate.

And it is undeniable that social capital, whoever defines it, is metaphoric to some extent. At any rate, Bourdieu's social capital resides in the upper class, not the whole of society, being transferrable through the generations and incarnate in other forms of capital.

Putnam: social capital as both public and private good

Affected significantly by Coleman rather than Bourdieu, Robert D. Putnam suggests a popular concept of social capital, defining it as "connections among individuals – social networks and the norms of reciprocity and trustworthiness that arise from them" (Putnam 2000: 19). He here seems to anchor social capital to network-basedness. But on numerous occasions he suggests diverse and even conflicting renditions of it. For example, he states, "Social capital is what the social philosopher Albert O. Hirschman calls a 'moral resource'" (Putnam 1994: 10); "Unlike conventional capital, social capital is a 'public good,' that is, it is not the private property of those who benefit from it" (1994: 10); "Social capital can thus be simultaneously a 'private good' and a 'public good'" (Putnam 2000: 20); "the performance of government and other social institutions is powerfully influenced by citizen engagement in community affairs, or what (following Coleman 1990) I termed social capital" (Putnam 1995: 664); "social trust and civic engagement are strongly correlated" (1995: 665); "Social capital ... refers to features of social organization, such as trust, norms, and networks, that can improve the efficiency of society by facilitating coordinated actions" (Putnam, Leonardi, and Nanetti 1993: 167). In short, Putnam's social capital can be a metaphoric moral resource, exclusively a public good at one point in time, but both private and public goods at another, as well as citizen engagement, trust, and, in the end, the overall embodiment of social organization. Notwithstanding or thanks to this catchall nature of social capital, his social capital has become the most well known.

Besides the criticism of its conceptual inconsistency, we need to ascertain the main characteristics of Putnam's social capital. Most of all, his social capital largely concerns outcomes at the macro level, such as economic development, democracy, livable community, or civil society. As detailed in chapter 2, the representative measures he employs with regard to social capital are the number of memberships in civic organizations and the generalized trust toward most people in a society, demonstrating that he is keen on collective results begotten by social capital. In other words, he is less interested in individual outcomes such as obtaining degrees and jobs or personal well-being, although there is no reason to suppose that he would be surprised if social capital produced those outcomes at the micro level (again, recall that he occasionally regards social capital as both private and public goods). Second, Putnam theorizes social capital to be a composite of multiple social and psychological traits, not a singular entity. This is shown in the way he conceptualizes it as a mixture of networks, norms of reciprocity, and trust, the first of which provides a structure for the latter two, while the latter two dictate normative and psychological rules of social, economic, and political exchanges. This is similar to how Coleman described social capital as composed of both social structure and functional actions. This multipronged approach differentiates him from, among others, Fukuyama, who emphasizes the normative feature of trust-infused culture, and Lin, who concentrates on the structural embeddedness of social resources. Third, path dependence, which roughly means those who take a particular path shall succeed whereas others on hopeless paths fail, is another feature of Putnam's social capital. Specifically, social capital in certain regions or nations is prone to grow, as if some hidden high interest rates were applied, while in others it is stagnant or even depreciates, largely due to historical and cultural legacies. In particular, his study of Italy's regional stratification in the growth of democracy and economy shows that northern regional polities, such as Tuscany and Emilia-Romagna, succeeded in public management and economic development but southern counterparts, like Sicily and Calabria, failed (Putnam, Leonardi, and Nanetti 1993). The crucial cause of the northern success, according to Putnam and his colleagues, is the historic legacy of civic community dating back to the eleventh century. It then happened that the lack of such civic infrastructure and voluntary cooperation among its citizens brought about the south's downfall. Highlighting the path-dependent nature of social capital, Putnam and colleagues claim, "Stocks of social capital, such as trust, norms, networks, tend to be self-reinforcing and cumulative ... Conversely, the absence of these traits in the *un*civic community is also self-reinforcing" (Putnam, Leonardi, and Nanetti 1993: 177). Logically, this path dependency may also predetermine the fate of uncivic nations that do not have the appropriate history and culture of social capital observed in the United States and some Western European countries. Even in the United States, Putnam argues that the stock of social capital has declined steeply, mainly because of the joint effects of (1) the decreasing proportion of civic generation (birth cohorts between 1910 and 1940), and (2) the spread of the television-watching culture (Putnam 1995, 1996, 2000).

Fukuyama: social capital as culture of trust

In regard to the path-dependent nature of social capital, Francis Fukuyama (1995a) has a strong affinity with Putnam because his theory is also founded on the historical and cultural makeup of a society. Most of all, he focuses on the width of trust people have toward others. Simply put, the width (or radius) here indicates how far one's trust range reaches. And trust and its radius are not easy to change for they are engrained in the culture of sociability. This culture of sociability – the ability to get along with other human beings – is accumulated over generations and learned informally. So he even maintains that social capital is part of human capital: "the component of human capital that allows members of a given society to trust one another and cooperate in the formation of new groups and associations" (Fukuyama 1995b: 90). His major argument is that nations with a familistic culture tend to confine spontaneous associations of their peoples within a small radius of families and clans, while peoples in non-kinship-based societies are prone to form wider associations, including those far beyond familial boundaries. He then goes on to categorize low-trust (i.e., China, France, Italy, and South Korea) and high-trust countries (Japan and Germany). A fundamental reason why it is hard to shift from, say, a low- to high-trust nation is that it requires unprecedented historical, cultural, social, political, or religious settings that are believed to be conducive to a trustful society: "Acquisition of social capital ... requires habituation to the moral norms of a community and ... the acquisition of virtues like loyalty, honesty, and dependability" (Fukuyama 1995a: 26–7); "Social capital is like a ratchet that is more easily turned in one direction than another; it can be dissipated by the actions of governments much more readily than those governments can build it up again" (1995a: 362). At the macro level, he maintains that the success of democratic capitalism depends on trust, an innate cultural feature (Fukuyama 2001, 2002). In conclusion, Fukuyama regards trust as a synonym for social capital: "Social capital is a capability that arises from the prevalence of trust in a society or in certain parts of it" (1995a: 26). What makes Fukuyama distinct from Putnam is that, among other things, he does not take a multipronged approach to social capital, concentrating solely on trust and its relevant moral norms rooted in varied cultures. For example, structural features such as networks do not occupy a place in Fukuyama's social capital. Therefore, his social capital theory bears a possibility of cultural determinism: "Social capital, the crucible of trust and critical to the health of an economy, rests on cultural roots" (Fukuyama 1995a: 33). Akin to Putnam's social capital, Fukuyama's is mainly related to macro-level collective outcomes such as democracy, economic development, or global economic organization. Another similarity between them is that both warn of the decline of social capital in the United States (e.g., Fukuyama 1995b).

Lin: social capital as embedded resources in social networks

Nan Lin theorizes social capital based strictly on interpersonal networks and resources attached to them, a partial resemblance to Coleman's approach that stressed interpersonal relations among other things. For instance, no norms of reciprocity are considered together with network resources. Neither does trust nor trustworthiness possess any portion in the network-based social capital. Specifically, Lin defines social capital as "embedded resources in social networks" (2001: 19) or "resources embedded in a social structure that are accessed and/or mobilized in purposive actions" (2001: 29). In short, for Lin, social capital is a form of capital captured through social relations. Lin thus differs from Putnam due to his monistic network-based approach to social capital, whereas Putnam has plural components to organize it, including networks. Also, he is quite distinct from Fukuyama because his social capital is embedded in social structure composed of relations among people, while Fukuyama's is entrenched in the cultural dimension of trust.

This structural approach to social capital stems from the literature of stratification and status attainment (Blau and Duncan 1967; Featherman and Hauser 1976; Featherman, Jones, and Hauser 1975; Lin 1999a; Lipset and Bendix 1959; Sewell, Haller, and Portes 1969). The stratification literature was mainly interested in what promotes or hinders mobility through status attainment within and across generations. Specifically, the literature concentrated on tracking intergenerational mobility trends among farm, manual, and nonmanual occupations, often using mobility tables and pertinent statistical methods. This indicates that mobility hinges largely on family background and cognitive ability transferred intergenerationally. In so doing, education (human capital) was conjointly added to explain more variation in social mobility (e.g., Blau and Duncan 1967; Breen and Jonsson 2005; Haveman and Smeeding 2006; Sewell, Haller, and Portes 1969; Treiman and Yip 1989). Then the role of social relations – particularly the effect of weakly related ties – became a focal concern in seeking to improve the status-attainment model on top of what had already been explained (Granovetter 1973, 1974). It is in this tradition of literature that Lin's social capital idea was conceived. Specifically, he is most interested in the possible socioeconomic mobility differentials created by social ties and their attendant information, influence, and power which in the incipient period were called social resources (Lin, Ensel, and Vaughn 1981; Lin, Vaughn, and Ensel 1981) and then later termed social capital (Lin 1999a, 2001). Therefore, Lin's social capital mainly concerns instrumental actions and personal gains through the use of social ties. Considering that Lin's social capital tends to expand through weak ties, those who are adventurous and socialize with unfamiliar and diverse others tend to accumulate greater social capital than those who hunker down with well-known and trusted ties alone. Thus the relationship between Lin's social capital and trust may not be positively linear, another demarcation from Putnam whose social capital subsumes trust organically. Nor does Lin's social capital subscribe to the path dependence of history and culture, another key difference to Putnam and Fukuyama.

Collective and individual social capital

Thus far, we have observed how several scholars, from Karl Marx to Nan Lin, produced their own versions of social capital concepts and theories. There can be palpable intellectual lineages, such as that from Coleman to Putnam and Fukuyama or another from the Marxian concept of capital to its variations found in Lin and Bourdieu. It is also plausible that Simmel's and Homans's emphasis on dyadic or triadic social relations in small groups is in line with Coleman's ideation of social capital composed of personal interactions in closed communities. In turn, this affected Lin's theorization of network-based social capital. A significant difference is that Lin's social capital is distributed across a whole social structure, whereas Coleman's is confined within a communal boundary. Among these diverse perspectives, similarities and differences coexist. And some differences are almost irreconcilable. For instance, trust, a cultural-historical legacy at the national or regional level, as well as a psychological trait at the individual level, is a key ingredient of social capital for Fukuyama and Putnam, whereas it is irrelevant to the social capital of Lin. Regarding the role of social networks, connectedness among persons is a necessary property of social capital in Putnam, while it is the quintessence of social capital in Lin and Bourdieu. However, what matters to Fukuyama is whether a collectivity has grown a culture and history of instantiated informal norms of cooperation, a synonym for social capital. Thus Fukuyama does not take social networks into account in theorizing social capital.

Notwithstanding such divergences, I suggest classifying two types of social capital: individual and collective. Lin also acknowledges that there can be a typology of social capital at the relational and group levels by mainly considering for whom – a specific individual in network or a collectivity as a whole? – the returns of purposive actions are accrued (Lin 1999b). In a similar vein, Poortinga (2006b) reports that individual social capital (i.e., trust and civic participation at the individual level) is more strongly related to the health of individuals compared to collective social capital (i.e., aggregated trust and civic participation at the national level). There are several relevant indicators of these two types of social capital, such as agency, projected objectives, and measurement of them, and the level of analysis as depicted in Table 1.1. As shown in the table, theorists conceptualize social capital at either the collective or individual level or both. Specifically, Marx, Bourdieu, and Fukuyama propose that social capital exists at the level of large collectivities, such as nation-state or social class, regardless of their mutually distinct approaches. Next, Coleman and Putnam develop flexible theorization of social capital going back and forth between interpersonal networks and collectivities. In contrast, Lin mainly conceptualizes network-based social capital that produces returns to individual actors, not to a whole community or a nation, although he also tries to expand this individual social capital formed at the relational level to the domain of civic actions and volunteerism (Son and Lin 2008). Thus Lin is the only theorist among the six whose social capital resides solely within interpersonal networks, while other scholars either stipulate social capital as collective assets, such as the total volume of individual capitals (Marx), the aggregated resources of the ruling class (Bourdieu), and the cultural and historical legacy of informal norms (Fukuyama), or straddle both the collective and individual sides of it (Coleman and Putnam). As a result, collective or group-level social capital is widespread in literature and among practitioners because most theorists pitch the concept of social capital at the collective level, even when some of them attribute its source to social networks at the micro level.

Likewise, the agencies also differ by key theorist. In Marx, it is capitalists. According to Bourdieu, it is the ruling class as a whole. In the case of Fukuyama, it is nation-states. For Lin, it cannot be impersonal entities but individuals belonging to networks. On the other hand, Coleman and Putnam do not specify agencies. They can be either individuals or organizations or, sometimes, nation-states. Similarly, measurement of agency, projected objectivities and their measurement, and major levels of analysis may differ according to different theorists as specified in the table and discussed at length in the previous section.

In particular, regarding the measurement of agency, the primary reason why we do not see much proliferation of Marxist or Bourdieuian concepts of social capital in research and practice is because it is hard to measure if and how individual capitals are aligned to form a nationally integrated capital (Marx), and it is also difficult to measure the presence and volume of institutionalized network constellations within a ruling class (Bourdieu). In the opposite sense, collective social capital proposed by Putnam and Coleman is most widespread, and yet relevant empirical studies based on the two theorists tend to lack consistency in measuring what social capital is; some regard generalized trust as social capital; others, hours with neighbors for schmoozing; others, voter-turnout rates in elections; others, individual memberships in voluntary associations; still others, the numbers of voluntary associations or NGOs in a country. Fukuyama's social capital is mostly measured by trust radius or generalized trust at the nation-state level. However, it is unclear if trust alone can indeed be the "instantiated informal norm" that creates cooperation among people. Lin's social capital is measured by the extensity of an individual network and its embedded resources, exemplifying the relational and interpersonal nature of his social capital. Despite being clear and consistent in measurement, its narrow application to the fields of status attainment and social mobility renders it more relevant to private goods than public goods. The next chapter discusses the measurement of individual and collective social capital in more detail.

This division between collective and individual social capital may not be perfect in the sense that theorists did not specifically envisage such categorization when they developed the concept. It may be the reason that Coleman and Putnam cross the boundary freely so that readers need to exert extra effort to establish in certain cases whether they deem social capital as a personal or group resource. However, the categorization, though made *ex post facto*, clears up confusion that stems from the lack of understanding in regard to what social capital specifically indicates, if and how it generates outcomes benefiting an individual or a collectivity among whom (or which) it resides, and who (or what) reproduces it. The typology of individual and collective social capital enables us to see some innate differences among theorists and also to appreciate commonalities between some multiple approaches, if not all.

Conclusion and what follows next

Long story short, no consensus exists as to what social capital is. Therefore, it is imperative to categorize varied usages of the term in a sensible way. I adopt the typology between individual and collective social capital in this book. Whenever necessary and possible in the forthcoming chapters, I refer to this categorization and particular theoretical backgrounds that helped form some specific applications of social capital. Before proceeding to empirical applications of social capital, we first need to know how those empirical studies measured the concept. Thus chapter 2 introduces the measurement of social capital. In particular, individual social capital has been measured by three generators of social network information – name, position, and resource generators. Collective social capital has had various ad hoc measures applied to it, such as membership in voluntary groups or generalized trust.

On the basis of the theoretical and methodological discussions, I present how the concept of social capital has been applied to several important substantive areas. Specifically, chapter 3 identifies the relationship between social capital, civil society, and development. The relevant empirical researchers mostly base their studies on the perspective of collective social capital, given that they hope to explain how to grow civic engagement and economic, social, and political development in nation-states. Chapter 4 concentrates on how social capital promotes intra- and intergenerational mobility and status attainment. This is a representative area where individual social capital embedded in interpersonal networks produces positive externalities for actors. Chapter 5 shifts the attention to a burgeoning research field that centers on the relationship between social capital and health. In this area, both collective and individual social capital is found to be associated with health outcomes, taking other likely causes of health into account. Chapter 6 details the expansion of social relations to cybernetworks, due to flourishing social networking services in the twenty-first century. This new online communication mode, conjoined with personalized wireless handheld devices, paved an alternative way to strengthen, reproduce, or, in some sense, exploit social capital.

The final chapter discusses the intellectual challenges that the social capital literature needs to overcome and proposes specifically how to empower the theory and concept of social capital. I suggest that the empowerment of social capital theory would be plausible if certain delimitations were critically applied to its various versions. The proposal to differentiate individual and collective social capital may be one reasonable way. Further, I also suggest that cultural-institutional preconditions that mold certain types of social relations need to be independently conceptualized from social capital. These demarcations may bring orderliness to and empower social capital in theory and practice.

2
Measuring Social Capital

It may be somewhat unusual for those who are versed in the social capital literature that this book discusses measurement in the second chapter. Above all, the measurement of social capital is a glaring weakness in the literature. This is largely because, as pointed out in the previous chapter, social capital does not have one single definition agreed by various scholars and disciplines. This lack of consensus has resulted in a wide array of social capital measures so that it is hard to organize them. Specifically, measures range from daily contact with neighbors to spending social nights with friends to membership in voluntary associations to whether or not a person trusts family, friends, or people in general. Still, measuring a concept using valid and reliable indicators is crucial in that it enables us, among other things: (1) to substantiate it in abstraction in the form of observable indicators so that its valid pertinence as a social reality can be either identified or falsified; (2) to appraise what personal, communal, societal, or national characteristics it is more likely to be associated or dissociated with; and (3) to relate such indicators of a concept to those of other concepts of interest to see if they are systematically related – for instance, if there is a strong relationship between social capital and health (the theme of chapter 5) – and, if so, in which direction – e.g., does social capital increase health or the other way around? Therefore, without proper measurement of a concept, the literature is less likely to grow coherently and further expand its applicability to other theoretical concepts.

As discussed in the preceding chapter, various concepts of social capital can be categorized into individual and collective types. Bearing in mind that individual social capital is based on personal networks and their accompanying features, it has engendered more concrete and specific measurement tools and indicators than has collective social capital. In particular, individual social capital has mostly been measured by network generators called name, position, and resource generators. The latter two indicate individual social capital as social resources that can be shared among the members of a network, whereas the first manifests the network and sociodemographic characteristics of intimate ties. By contrast, collective social capital has not had its own measurement methods; that is, no systematic generator of it exists in the literature. And yet various ad hoc indicators have been employed in accordance with how different versions of collective social capital emphasize certain aspects of sociality.

This chapter details how the two types of social capital have been measured in the literature. It begins with individual social capital because it has specific measurement methods based on interpersonal networks. All three network generators – name, position, and resource generators – are discussed in terms of their content, major characteristics, and limitations. In regard to the measurement of collective social capital, the discussion sheds light on two representative indicators – trust toward people and membership in voluntary associations. These two staple measures of collective social capital have been frequently used in a variety of contexts. I also introduce variants of these two measures, as well as some alternative indicators.

Measures of individual social capital

Individual social capital is also called network-based social capital. There are two reasons. First, social networks are a sort of structural web composed of both nodes of agents and the presence or absence of mutual ties connecting them.

Second, the structural web holds a variety of resources belonging to the agents and makes the shared resources available for those who need them. Such network-basedness of individual social capital necessitated the development of network generators to measure how resourceful a network is. A name generator, the first network generator that appeared in the literature, aims to capture a core-discussion network composed of people close to an individual. Resources shared in name-generator networks are usually empathy and emotional support, although the exchange of material goods and services is also possible. A position generator measures the number of job holders in the labor market from which the size and diversity of a network can be assessed. A resource generator elucidates the specific content of resources which can actually be provided by people belonging to a network. Such contents include information, skills, and material assets. It is now time to get to know the three network generators of individual social capital in more detail.

Name generator

Who do you rely on when you encounter a certain issue that matters to you but you are unsure of how to deal with it alone? These issues can vary from person to person. Also, a person tends to experience a variety of problems across the life course – childhood, youth, adulthood, marriage, separation, divorce, parenting, getting old, critical illness, and impending death. A name generator sheds light on a few or several persons around the focal person who are at least willing to understand what those issues are, whether or not they are actually able to help. Thus Marsden (1987) calls it a "core-discussion network." The core-discussion network comprises a few or several names provided by a focal person (or *ego* as it is usually called in the social network literature) so that the method is labeled a "name generator." A name-generator section appeared in the 1985 General Social Survey (GSS), a representative national survey in America. Specifically, the lead question in a name generator is this: "From time to time, most people discuss important matters with other people. Looking back over the last six months – who are the people with whom you discussed matters important to you? Just tell me their first names or initials" (Marsden 1987: 123). The reason why "discuss important matters" was chosen as the key criterion for the generator was due to the "view that influence processes and normative pressures operate through intimate, comparatively strong ties" (Marsden 1987: 123; refer to Burt 1984). Thus, in principle, a name generator is designed to capture strong and intimate ties around an ego. Mainly concerned with the people surrounding the focal person, this method is properly called "egocentric." The respondents then get a further request to answer questions about the first five names they offer. In particular, these name-interpreter questions reveal a respondent's degree of closeness to each person named (or *alter* as it is usually called in the social network literature), frequency of contact, the length of the relationship, as well as the age, sex, race, and religion of each of them. Further probed is the presence or absence of a relationship between each pair of alters (or people in a network).

The name generator has a long tradition in the literature as detailed by Small (2017: 12–16). It was Lazarsfeld who devised a way to get some names of people around a respondent who, for instance, influenced their opinions or were trustworthy regarding public issues (Katz and Lazarsfeld 1955). These people are called opinion leaders in communication studies. Laumann (1973) also used a name generator that aimed to find out the three closest friends of a respondent. Similarly, Wellman, in his East Yorkers study in Canada, asked for the names of the six closest intimates ("the persons outside your home that you feel closest to") that comprised egocentric intimate networks (1979: 1208–9). Then Fischer (1982) applied eleven types of name generator to a sample of Northern Californians, asking, for example, for the names of people whom a respondent discussed personal matters with, consulted for important decisions, talked to about hobbies, and so forth. Influenced by Fischer's approach, Burt (1984) wanted to include a section of name generator in the aforementioned 1985 GSS. In order to save survey time and money, he had to choose just one type of name generator and thus selected "discussing important matters" – note that he replaced Fischer's discussing "personal matters" with discussing "important matters" – as the key criterion. And this core-discussion network has since been adopted in numerous surveys and studies (e.g., Campbell and Lee 1991 [US]; Boase and Ikeda 2012 [Japan]; Mollenhorst, Völker, and Flap 2008 [Netherlands]; Ruan 1998 [China]; Völker and Flap 2001 [Germany]).

All in all, the name generator of a core-discussion network has been assumed to produce information regarding close and intimate alters around an ego. And it is also likely that the ego (focal person) reciprocates relations of closeness and intimacy to those named. Although identifying five named persons is limiting because they may be just a small fraction of a network, some believe that a name generator can be useful for indicating the richness or paucity of social relations. So, for example, McPherson and his colleagues (McPherson, Smith-Lovin, and Brashears 2006) argued that Americans suffer from social isolation due to a decrease in the number of close alters over two decades, as measured by the 1985 and 2004 General Social Surveys, the two occasions on which the GSS included a name-generator section. Specifically, they reported that the average core-discussion network size decreased from about three in 1985 to two in 2004, while the number of people who had no one with whom to discuss important matters tripled. This striking finding on social isolation is in line with Robert Putnam's (2000) argument for declining social capital which caught media attention. The *Washington Post*, for example, reported that Putnam commented, "the new study supports what he has been saying for years to skeptical audiences in the academy" (Vedantam 2006). However, the study was submitted to scrutiny and provoked hot debate. And it was found that the results indicating social isolation may be artificial because there were serious problems, such as interviewer effect (meaning that some survey interviewers prompted passive or even no responses to the name-generator section from interviewees in order to finish surveys early), interview fatigue (the tediousness of the name-generator section discouraged complete responses to it), and survey design effect (the location of the name-generator section in the survey affected the response rate) (Fischer 2009; McPherson, Smith-Lovin, and Brashears 2009; Paik and Sanchagrin 2013). Further, in contrast to the argument about social isolation and declining social capital, Wellman (2012) estimates that, with the help of the internet, an average American has 610 network connections, a significant portion of them intimate and close.

Another challenge came from Small's (2017) study with regard to who these persons in core-discussion networks are. Rather than strong ties, what he found is that a significant proportion of core-discussion networks comprise weakly related persons. These weak ties are acquaintances, such as miscellaneous co-workers, who are not particularly close but are willing to lend their ears. Sometimes they can be strangers in the next seat on a flight. It is possible that some sensitive issues, such as mental illness or sexual assault, are, people feel, hard to share with family and close friends. Or people tend to discuss important matters with whoever is around at that moment. Therefore, Small argues that the unilateral assumption that a name generator produces only strong and intimate ties around an ego may need to be reconsidered. Additionally, the perception of "important matters" may differ from person to person. Bearman and Parigi (2004), looking specifically at this matter, found that people talked about less important things, such as the cloning of headless frogs or eating habits.

Despite these weaknesses and complications, the name generator is regarded as a representative network generator. And its contribution to the empirical understanding of what the network of core discussion looks like, who these network alters are, and how the network alters are connected or unconnected should be duly acknowledged.

Position generator

By now, you may have a sense of what network generators can or cannot do. In fact, it is impossible for any network generator to grasp the totality of a network. Rather, each network generator provides partial information regarding a particular aspect of some, though not all, persons in a network. A name generator, for example, produces the names of several people in a network. Likewise, a position generator shows what kinds of job these network alters possess. That is, a position generator introduces some members of a network in terms of their positions in the labor market. Yet there are critical differences between name and position generators. First, the presence or absence of hierarchy among network alters is a key difference between them. For instance, no hierarchy exists between names such as Bob and Richie or Diane and Julie in principle. Of course, names that evoke race may induce favor or discrimination in daily interactions or job searches (Bertrand and Mullainathan 2004). Nonetheless, the hierarchical ordering of names other than alphabetical arrangement is impossible. However, job titles are not free from status comparisons. To wit, people can easily discern which of a pair of jobs (e.g., lawyer/cleaner or banker/construction worker) is higher in terms of economic reward and social prestige. Therefore, knowing job titles by implementing a position generator is closely related to getting access to the hierarchical composition of a network. The other substantive difference is that a position generator can garner a greater number of known ties because there is no limit enforced, such as a maximum of five names. Usually 10–20 job titles are put to respondents by a position generator.

The position generator was conceived by Nan Lin and Mary Dumin in the mid-1980s (Lin and Dumin 1986). They suggested that positions (jobs) in occupational structures involve a variety of resources. Then they posited that a person gets access through his or her social ties to occupational positions with resources. Specifically, they asked if a respondent knew any of 20 job holders belonging to upper-white, lower-white, upper-blue, and lower-blue collar occupational groups. These jobs were selected based on "the frequency distributions of occupations of the American labor force from the 1970 Census of Population, Classified Index of Occupations" (Lin and Dumin 1986: 371). Specifically, the position generator asks whether any of one's relatives, friends, or acquaintances (people who know each other by face and name) has one of the occupations listed. The answer must be a simple yes or no. Where several acquaintances have the same job, the respondent is advised to answer regarding the first person who springs to mind. After the respondent answers all the position items, occupational prestige scores or socioeconomic index (SEI) scores are allocated to the known positions. For example, an SEI score of 92 is given to a lawyer and a score of 17 to a bartender (Lin and Dumin 1986). These responses to position-generator items are then used to draw up indicators of social resources. They are extensity (number of job holders known), upper reachability (occupational prestige or SEI score of the highest job title known), and range of prestige (the gap in occupational prestige or SEI scores between the highest and lowest job titles). In later studies, these three indicators are sometimes merged as a single variable that accounts for the volume, highest status accessed, and diversity of occupational ties altogether (Lin 2001; Lin, Fu, and Hsung 2001).

Most of all, parsimony is a comparative merit in a position generator. As mentioned, the respondents may simply answer yes or no to a series of position items (e.g., do you know a computer programmer?). Other subsidiary information, such as gender, race, marital status, or the educational level of each position holder can be probed, although it may be excised in order to reduce survey time and cost. The mutual relations between position holders are not established. Because the position generator enables comparison of volume, resourcefulness, and degree of occupational diversity in networks, it has a distinct advantage over the name generator.

Nonetheless, a position generator has its own setbacks. First, people who do not have work status in the labor market are significantly disadvantaged because they will not know as many job holders as those currently working. This disadvantage applies, in particular, to the unemployed, the laid-off, the retired, and full-time students and housewives. Second, position-generator items need to be adjusted according to the socioeconomic contexts in which respondents are situated. Proportions of various positions in an occupational structure may differ according to levels of national development. That is, computer programmers are easily included in a friendship network in Silicon Valley, whereas they are rare in Sierra Leone where the majority of the population works in agriculture and mining. Further, even within a nation there can be disproportionate distribution of positions. For example, Matous and Ozawa (2010) find that in general position-generator items cannot be applied to slum dwellers in the Philippines. People with low levels of education and income felt intimidated when asked if they knew high-position holders such as lawyers. Therefore, the list of positions had to be changed to include largely low-prestige jobs. In addition, the number of positions asked about had to be reduced, due to the short attention span of the slum dwellers. Third, a position generator may induce various recall errors by respondents. For example, Van der Gaag, Appelhof, and Webber (2011) find that interviewees reported unfamiliarity with occupations such as "foreman," "mechanic," and "information technologist." Many interviewees also admitted forgetting alters. In addition, confusion concerning the occupation of alters caused the same alters to be listed under different occupations. Fourth, it is assumed that occupational positions are a crucial basis of social resources without clarifying what specific types of resource are available to the focal person in a network. Various resources, such as job information, influence, and power, are supposed to be provided by a positional network. However, it is uncertain which of them is actually exchanged.

Despite such weaknesses, a position generator is regarded as an efficient tool for sampling the network ties of respondents. Above all, a position generator fits well with the concept of social capital because it captures job titles possessed by social ties that are hierarchically ordered in the occupational structure, which enables the calculation of the amount and diversity of socioeconomic resources. Nonetheless, its limitations as detailed above resulted in the formation of a third type of network generator.

Resource generator

The resource generator is the latest addition to the family of network generators. It is a Dutch invention (Van der Gaag and Snijders 2005), designed to overcome the disadvantages of the name generator (e.g., burdensome interview process, redundant data regarding multiple alters) and the position generator (e.g., lack of specific details about resources and their diversity). At the same time, it aims to retain the merits of the name generator (e.g., detailed descriptions of social ties) and the position generator (e.g., easy to administer).

Specifically, a resource generator has the same question-naire structure as a position generator. The difference is that a resource generator presents respondents with a fixed list of resources, rather than occupations, and asks if they know anyone who would give access to a particular resource. They are also asked to indicate the tie strength (i.e., acquaintance, friend, or family) between them and their ties. However, unlike a name generator, the resource generator does not ask name-interpreter questions. As a result, the generator is quick to administer, yet gives a "clear referral to specific social resources" (Van der Gaag and Snijders 2005: 4).

Its exemplary questions are as follows. Do you know anyone who "owns a holiday home abroad?", "has knowledge about financial matters (taxes, subsidies)?", "can speak and write a foreign language?", or "can give a good reference when applying for job?" These four questions are representative items of prestige and education related social capital, political and financial skills social capital, personal skills social capital, and personal support social capital, respectively. Therefore, a resource generator produces multi-dimensional social capital scales based on numerous questions probing particular resources such as material assets, profes-sional knowledge, various skills, and willingness to provide instrumental and expressive support when in need. The other two generators do not offer such detailed information concerning the various kinds of resources belonging to network alters. Thus Van der Gaag and Snijders (2005) call the resource generator a measure of "general" social capital. This means that the multidimensional social capital produced by a resource generator is applicable to the population in general, not merely a particular segment of it such as those in the labor market who are likely to know more occupation holders in the position generator than those outside it.

However, a resource generator does have weaknesses. A critical limitation is that it does not inform us of the number of ties that provide the resources. In an extreme case, it is possible that the same person owns a holiday home, is knowl-edgeable about financial matters, speaks and writes a foreign language, and gives a good reference for a job. This problem stems from the non-specificity of the number of ties. In other words, a resource generator produces information with regard to the volume and diversity of the shared resources in a network but not to the number of persons belonging to the network or who they are. Second, a resource generator lacks international comparability. In particular, the resource items and the multidimensional scales of social capital may differ from country to country due to the idiosyncratic sociocultural and political economic features of various nations. There is no guarantee, for instance, that the prestige and education related social capital found in the Netherlands is applicable to, say, Mexico; in fact, prestige and education might make separate scales of social capital in some countries. In short, lacking international comparability, resource-generator items need to be developed anew, or at least revised, for each country. Third, its multidimensionality renders the concept of social capital too broad so that its clarity suffers. For example, personal support social capital is similar to social support, a pre-established concept. The scale includes items such as knowing "anyone who can give advice about conflict at work or with family members." These can be regarded as typical indicators of social support in medical sociology (Cobb 1976; Sherbourne and Stewart 1991), although some researchers view social support as a form of social capital (Carpiano 2006). Thus its multidimensionality makes social capital less coherent. Fourth, even though it is argued that a resource-generator produces social capital applicable to the general population, socioeconomic features such as education, occupational prestige, and belonging to the labor market were associated with a higher volume of overall social capital (Van der Gaag and Snijders 2005: 18).

With respect to the second limitation of international comparability, Webber and Huxley (2007) developed a new list of resource items suited to the target population in the United Kingdom. A similar endeavor has been made in the United States by Foster and Maas (2016) who devised a list of 21 resource items called the RG-US (Resource Generator-United States). In the end, those items formed three dimensions: namely, expert access, personal support, and problem-solving social capital. In addition, Griep et al. (2013) dropped four items from the original resource list proposed by Van der Gaag and Snijders (2005) in order to make it applicable to Brazil. These studies verify that no

Table 2.1 Individual social capital

Measurement Tool	Specifics	Strength	Weakness
Name generator	Respondents are typically asked the following question: "From time to time, most people discuss important matters with other people. Looking back over the last six months – who are the people with whom you discussed matters important to you?" (Marsden 1987:123). For the first five names listed, respondents are also requested to complete name interpreter questions (e.g., degree of closeness, age, sex, race)	Captures information regarding close and intimate alters surrounding ego. Can indicate the number of intimate ties. Indicators of network features may be constructed: – network size – network density – network heterogeneity	Elucidates only a small fraction of a respondent's network. Can cause fatigue for respondents due to a series of follow-up network interpreter questions. The perception of "important matters" may vary among respondents.
Position generator	A random list of 10–20 job titles is presented to respondents and they are asked to indicate if they know any relatives, friends, and acquaintances who hold the listed jobs.	Reveals the hierarchical composition of a network. Easy to administer. Indicators of social resources may be constructed: – extensity (network size; network diversity) – upper reachability – range of prestige	Respondents not in the labor market are disadvantaged as they may not be acquainted with as many job holders. Has to be adjusted according to cross-national socioeconomic contexts. Respondents may be unfamiliar with job titles. Does not clarify what specific resources are available to the respondent other than the occupational status attached to the jobs.
Resource generator	Respondents are given a list of resources and asked if they know anyone who could provide access to each resource (e.g., Do you know anyone who "can speak or write a foreign language", "can give a good reference when applying for job?")	Provides detailed information regarding the specific resources available through the network. Easy to administer. Indicators of social resources may be constructed: – prestige and education related social capital – political and financial skills social capital – personal skills social capital – personal support social capital	Does not make clear the number of ties (number of persons) that provide resources. Multidimensionality may blur the concept of social capital. Lack of international comparability – resource-generator items may need to be revised for each country (e.g., RG-UK, RG-Japan).

one version of resource-generator items can be used in all countries.

As discussed thus far, all three network generators have comparative advantages and disadvantages. They are summarized in Table 2.1. No single one has absolute superiority over the others. The choice of generator depends on what type of network resource is the core interest. So nowadays researchers employ multiple network generators in surveys, as in the case of the recent ISSP (International Social Survey Program) 2017 module on Social Networks and Social Resources that includes both position and resource generators. On the whole, the crucial commonality among the three generators is that they are firmly based on individual social networks. It is impossible to conceive core-discussion alters (name generator), occupational positions of alters (position generator), and various resources attached to alters (resource generator) without the presence of ego-centered social networks. And this is the reason that these network generators are considered measures of network-based individual social capital.

Measures of collective social capital

Collective social capital does not necessitate individuals' participation in personal networks. For instance, once in a closely knit community, individuals who have not actually formed any specific ties to other residents can enjoy the benefits of communal bonding and resources. This is why Putnam (2000) gives an example of bystanders who did not join neighborhood activities or associations but got their homes protected by the community even when they were away on trips. In such communities, looking after their neighbor's home is an unspoken norm. Likewise, Coleman (1988) describes a mother who moved from Detroit to Jerusalem because she would not need to worry about the safety of her six young children when they went to school on a city bus or played in a neighborhood park without her presence. So collective social capital does not stress about particular connections between people at the micro level. Nor does it care about measuring personal connections. More important is whether and how much unspoken norms of reciprocity and trust are pervasive in a whole community. This is the reason why so-called generalized trust, that is, trust toward most people in a society, has become a key measure of collective social capital. In addition, although collective social capital does not usually take interpersonal connections into account, it does consider belonging to voluntary associations by the individuals to be important (Paxton 1999; Putnam 2000). The presumption is that those who care about community tend to either set up a voluntary association or participate in pre-established ones. Thus organizational belonging can be an indicator of the presence of social capital at the collective level. Most scholars who use voluntary associational membership in their studies call it a measure of social capital, not particularly *collective* social capital because network-based individual social capital does not matter much to them or is not so important as to be differentiated. We will now see how trust and organizational belonging have been used as measures of collective social capital.

Trust

In fact, trust, along with membership in voluntary associations, is one of the most frequently used indicators of social capital in the literature (Fukuyama 1995a; Newton 2001). Trust is a psychological trait that helps initiate social contacts, exchanges, and durable relations with other human beings. And such contacts, exchanges, and durable associations comprise social networks and social capital.

As the concept of social capital is manifold, so is trust (Uslaner 2008). Some researchers concentrate on the particular and relational nature of trust, while others emphasize its general and moral characteristic. While these two types of trust are directed at either particular or generalized people, trust can also be given to impersonal institutions. First, some scholars maintain that whether to trust or not is based on each person's rational calculation of the interests of the other parties (Hardin 1993, 2002, 2006). And the decision to trust or distrust is thus related to the knowledge and experiences of the same or similar cases in the past. In other words, it is distinct from vague expectations of how people in general think and behave. Rather, the decision involves deliberation to assess the level of trustworthiness of a particular person, considering whether the expected behavior fits that person's interest. So Yamagishi and Yamagishi (1994: 139) call it "knowledge-based trust," while Uslaner (2008: 102) names it "strategic trust" because the procedure involves selective decision and action. This type of trust can be given to, or sometimes taken away from, persons we know. In this regard, we may call it particular trust.

The second perspective takes people unknown to us into account. It is impossible to relate to all persons within a national boundary. Practically speaking, most people, except those we know, are in some sense an unknown mass. Regarding this huge group of unfamiliar people, we cannot tell how trustworthy each of them is. Therefore, a ballpark evaluation of trust toward the unspecified others is inevitable. For example, such an estimation is encouraged in the representative survey question of generalized trust that first appeared in Rosenberg's (1956: 690) scale of "faith in people": "Some people say that most people can be trusted. Others say you can't be too careful in your dealings with people. How do you feel about it?" As the name of the scale – faith in people – suggests, this second type of trust takes normative judgment of people more seriously than a specific reckoning of their trustworthiness. Thus Uslaner (2008: 103) argues that this second type of trust is a moralistic trust under the premise, "others share your fundamental moral values and therefore should be treated as you would wish to be treated by them." So this ballpark estimation is different from a utilitarian calculation of possible gains or losses from trusting someone. Rather, it is more closely related to a fundamental belief (or disbelief) in human nature. The situation gets even more complicated in the modern day when the internet has become an alternative communication channel that enables interactions even between total strangers. For example, Etzioni (2017) argues that the thriving e-commerce (e.g., eBay and Amazon) and online sharing economy (e.g., Uber and Lyft) would not exist if people did not put their trust in strangers as service providers and customers; how do you trust that the Uber driver, a complete stranger, would not harm you after you got in the vehicle? Basically, this off- and online trust in most people is the staple measure of social capital (Fukuyama 1995a; Putnam 2000). For instance, Kawachi and his colleagues (Kawachi, Kennedy, Lochner, and Prothrow-Stith 1997) found that generalized trust, a measure of social capital, is inversely related to mortality, mediating the effect of income inequality on mortality. In short, trusters tend to live longer. Also, Shah, Kwak, and Holbert (2001) reported that internet usage for information exchange is associated with generalized trust, an indicator of social capital, although internet usage for social recreation is unrelated to it. Thus what we do online may be related to whether we trust anonymous people. All in all, this second type of trust is called generalized trust.

Lastly, trust can be directed toward impersonal public institutions as people may hold different levels of confidence in government, legal institutions, media, companies, and nonprofit organizations. This third type of trust is a by-product of industrialization, the advent of which was closely associated with modern bureaucracy, regulation, and legislation (Zucker 1986). Due to the industrial revolution that originated in Europe and thereafter spread to North America, Asia, and Africa, people saw the unprecedented upspring of various corporate bodies. As a result, it became necessary for people to determine the trustworthiness of institutions in addition to the trustworthiness of particular and generalized others. For instance, there is a stark difference between people living under a predatory state or an autonomous state (Evans 1995); in the former, people need to devise tactics to avoid being exploited by the ruthless state, whereas in the latter people assume that they are protected by the state as long as they keep on the right side of the law. Just as we observe the variation in, say, generalized trust across nations, trust in institutions differs country by country. This third type of trust in impersonal institutions is often called institutional trust, as opposed to interpersonal trust.

Membership in voluntary associations

When Putnam (2000: 15–16) opened up his discussion on declining social capital in the United States in *Bowling*

Alone, he gave as examples the Glenn Valley Bridge Club (Pennsylvania) which had broken up, the National Association for the Advancement of Colored People's (NAACP) Roanoke chapter (Virginia), whose membership dwindled steeply in the 1990s, and the alumni of Vassar College of Washington, DC, who had to have their 51st and last annual book sale in 1999 for the college scholarships because volunteers were too old to continue any longer and, more critically, there were no new volunteers who would replace them. Thus, for Putnam, the reduction in the number of diverse community groups and their members was a crucial indication of diminishing social capital. And, of course, such reduction in community groups and volunteers is allegedly related to lower generalized trust. Why does the number of voluntary groups and individuals who belong to and engage with them matter? There are some significant answers to that question. First, in principle people establish formal and informal associations to pursue some specific collective goals (instrumentally driven grouping) and/or share common sentiments and interests among themselves (expressively driven grouping). Thus the presence of voluntary groups indicates the extent to which collective bonding, a synonym for social capital, flourishes in a society. Second, those social groups provide opportunities for initiating and enlarging social ties beyond individual network boundaries. You meet and befriend some persons in voluntary associations whom you would otherwise have slim chance of ever encountering in your daily life. So voluntary associations increase the likelihood of expanding social networks for their participants. Third, at the macro level, voluntary associations perform the role of public conduits through which various socioeconomic exchanges occur between those who give their time and resources and the recipients. This role may in some cases include the redistribution of wealth, which helps ameliorate overall inequality in communities or in a whole society. Fourth, voluntary associations may ignite macro-level social, economic, and political changes, as we can observe in various incidents such as Occupy Wall Street in the United States, the Arab Spring in the Middle East, and the Candlelight Revolution in South Korea. Therefore, in the opposite sense, lack of voluntary associations and of engaging members in them may suggest a low level of collective bonding, a smaller individual social network on average, a wider gap between the haves and have-nots, and less opportunities to beget macro-level social, economic, and political changes.

In practice, membership in voluntary associations has thus been employed as a measure of collective social capital. The basic assumption is that the greater the number of memberships in voluntary associations, the greater the social capital (Newton 1997; Paxton 1999; Putnam 2000, 2001; Wollebaek and Selle 2002). Usually, the researchers tally the number of memberships without differentiating the types and characteristics among the groups. That is, membership in a parent–teacher association (PTA) is treated equally with membership in a political party or an environmental organization. And yet even when the total number of undifferentiated memberships in sundry associations is considered, relevant studies have reported that this is positively related to civic engagement (Dekker and Van den Broek 1998), trust (Paxton 2007), health (Rietschlin 1998), development (Woolcock and Narayan 2000), and status attainment (Ruiter and De Graaf 2009).

Although the overall membership in associations matters significantly for various instrumental and expressive outcomes, some researchers have found that the types and internal characteristics of organizations have their own impacts as well. For instance, Stolle and Rochon (1998) compared seven types of voluntary associations (i.e., cultural, political, economic, group rights, community, personal interest, and social) in the United States, Sweden, and Germany and found that the cultural type is related to a wider range of social capital indicators, such as generalized trust, political trust and efficacy, and tolerance, than the other types. They further reported that the diversity of associations in regard to education, occupation, religion, partisanship, age, gender, race, and proportion of immigrants is positively related to generalized trust and communal exchange of credit slips, which is the opposite of what Putnam (2007) maintained with respect to the depreciating role of diversity against trust and social capital. Van der Meer and Grotenhuis (2009) suggested that there are three types of associations – leisure, interest, and activist organizations – and argued that lumping them together may cancel the effect of each on certain outcomes such as political action and trust in parliament. In addition, Diez de Ulzurrun (2002) pointed out that respondents are mostly asked to indicate the "types" of association they engage with but not how many groups within each type they belong to nor the names of the organizations. Further, an amorphous "other groups" category is often used to make up for the lack of detailed types of association.

In general, it is true that membership in voluntary associations has been employed frequently as a measure of collective social capital. And this measure seems adequate for the concept of collective social capital because it encapsulates the ties a person makes with collective entities, as opposed to ties to other individuals.

In sum, the representative measures of collective social capital include trust and membership in voluntary associations (see Table 2.2 for more details). Trust can roughly be divided into two actual measures: particular trust and generalized trust. In the literature, generalized trust has been more widely used as a measure. Generalized trust may be more fitted to the concept of collective social capital because it deals mainly with the trustworthiness of most people in a society. Next, membership in voluntary associations has frequently been used as a measure of collective social capital. Mostly, the overall number of memberships in voluntary associations has been a popular measure. Yet there have been some critical studies which suggest that the types of organization that people selectively join may matter more than the total count of membership in those types of association.

Conclusion

It may seem tedious to go through ways of measuring of social capital – actually, measurement of any concept can be boring to readers, more so if the concept does not have a fixed, consensual definition among researchers and practitioners. This is why it is necessary, as shown in the first chapter, to apply a bifurcated categorization to the concept so that we can at least take a holistic view

Table 2.2 Collective social capital

Indicator	Specifics	Strength	Weakness
Trust	General Trust: This is the typical question – "Generally speaking, would you say that most people can be trusted or that you can't be too careful in dealing with people?" Particular trust: Surveys may ask respondents if they trust a specific group of people. For instance, regarding trust of neighbors, respondents may be asked if they trust, "many of the people", "most of the people", "a few of the people", "or nobody else in their neighborhood" (Carpiano and Fitterer 2014: 228).	General trust takes unknown people into account. In other words, it evaluates the level of trust toward unspecified others and enables the measurement of the trustworthiness of most people in society. General trust has been used as a representative measure of collective social capital in the literature. Particular trust measures can be aggregated at ecological levels to form indicators of collective social capital (e.g., neighborhood trust, community trust).	It has been argued that while trust represents the willingness of a person to establish social ties, this psychological state or disposition to engage others is conceptually distinct from possessing social capital (Carpiano and Fitterer 2014). In answering the generalized trust question, it has been found that many respondents actually thought of people they know personally. Hence, general and particular trust may be overlapped.
Membership in voluntary associations	Respondents are typically given a list of associations (e.g., religious group, school association, sport club, skill or hobby group, professional association, political group, or labor union) and asked to indicate those of which they are members. The number of memberships is then tallied, and it is assumed that the greater the number of memberships, the greater the social capital.	As voluntary associations are established to pursue collective goals and/or share common sentiments and interests, membership in them indicates the extent to which collective bonding and bridging social capital flourishes in a society. Captures additional ties a person can make in collective entities, apart from those belonging to personal networks.	Respondents are usually asked to indicate the number of associational types they belong. However, the number of groups within each type is not considered in most cases. Also, the blanket measure of the number of memberships in voluntary associations is incapable of indicating diversity of organizational types. For instance, membership in a religious group should be qualitatively different from another membership in an environmental or political organization. The list of associational types needs to be tailored to countries that have different cultural backgrounds. Some countries may have types of association that are unique to them; for instance, fraternities are commonplace in America but "rare or nonexistent" elsewhere (De Ulzurrun 2002: 505).

of it and understand how it has been used in various substantive fields. This chapter thus followed the division between individual and collective social capital. The essential character of individual social capital is its network-basedness. This means that social resources, no matter what they indicate, cannot exist separate to interpersonal networks. In principle, the supporters of this conceptualization maintain, "no networks, no social capital." This stringent ideation of social capital is manifest in how it has been measured. That is, *network* generators were at the core of the measurement of individual social capital. What differentiates the three network generators that this chapter has introduced is the representative features captured by each generator: the name generator measures the personal identities of intimate ties and if and how they are mutually related; the position generator indicates how narrow or wide are the occupational locations of the known ties; and the resource generator pays particular attention to the presence and diversity of physical and nonphysical assets that may be provided by the network ties. Although the contents of interest – names, positions, and resources – differ from each other, they are all attached to the persons connected by a network. Therefore, in an extreme sense, social isolates who shut themselves off from other people should be devoid of any pooled capital that could have been formed and shared among ties in a network.

However clean-cut and crisp the tripartite measurement may seem, individual social capital is restricted in the sense that it focuses solely on the access to and utilization of instrumental and expressive assets – in the form of known names, positions, and miscellaneous resources – delimited in an *interpersonal* network. To wit, the benefits of individual social capital apply in principle only to persons who weave, maintain, or extend a social network. For this reason, the meaning of "social" in individual social capital can be somewhat narrow, denoting the co-ownership of resources only among those who belong to networks. That is, the ownership or the right to borrow or lend pooled resources does not usually go beyond the boundary of a network to anonymous outsiders. For that reason, individual social capital is effective in preventing free riders, which can be positive and negative concurrently; positive because it is cost-effective without wasting resources on non-participants but negative because its coverage extends only to network margins. Thus a specific network delimitation defines and measures individual social capital in clearer terms – of course, we need to understand that a person's whole network is not easy to measure and that network generators sample only a small part of it. Paradoxically, the network delimitation may be the reason why individual social capital has not been as popular in academia and among practitioners as collective social capital. In this regard, it is notable that all three generators of individual social capital were developed by sociologists – from Paul Lazarsfeld and Elihu Katz to Nan Lin to Martin Van der Gaag – and that the concept and measurement of individual social capital has been adopted mostly by a specific group of researchers specializing in social network studies.

In contrast, collective social capital does not particularly position itself in interpersonal networks, although sometimes networks are claimed as a core component of it (e.g., Putnam 2000). Nor is it concerned with how to delimit its scope. Instead, its main interest is in how to expand the scope of coverage at least to a community or in many cases to a whole country, as a result of which we see numerous comparative studies of collective social capital across nations (e.g., Delhey, Newton, and Welzel 2011; Fukuyama 1995a; Paxton 2002, 2007). Researchers of collective social capital tend to utilize two representative measures in regard to social capital: generalized trust, and the number of memberships in voluntary organizations. For instance, in defining social capital for an empirical comparative study of 48 countries, Paxton (2002: 256) stipulates, "Social capital requires (1) objective associations among individuals, and (2) associations of a particular type – reciprocal, trusting, and involving positive emotion." Then she goes on to measure the first aspect of association by the average number of respondents' voluntary association memberships in each country and the mean number of voluntary association memberships for which members have actually conducted voluntary work in the past year; and the second aspect of positive emotion by the percentage of respondents in each country who answered that they could trust most people. Although Paxton mentions "objective associations among individuals" in measuring social capital, it is obvious that she does not mean associations between individuals but the collective level of organizational associations. Likewise, positive emotion as a particular type of association does not indicate that a person trusts members in a network. Rather, it indicates trust in an anonymous mass of people in a whole society, most of whom are outside personal networks. Therefore, the boundary of collective social capital is wide open, without specific delimitation. So the implication of "social" in collective social capital is much broader than its counterpart in individual social capital. And it is not easy to distinguish between those who have a due share in collective social capital and those bystanders who only get the benefits without investing in it. Thus the presence of free riders is a more serious issue in collective social capital. Nonetheless, collective social capital is more flexible and amorphous in terms both of its conceptual definition and of measurement so that it has attracted greater attention from media, politics, international organizations, public health, and the voluntary sector.

It should be noted that qualitative approaches to social capital have also thrived, although they are not discussed in this chapter. They mainly focus on case studies (e.g., Kleinhans, Priemus, and Engbersen 2007; Melo Zurita et al. 2018; Svendsen and Svendsen 2004), participant observation (e.g., Anderson and Jack 2002; Ginwright 2007), in-depth interviews (e.g., Shpigelman 2018; Svendsen 2006), and triangulation between various methods (e.g., Dudwick, Kuehnast, Nyhan Jones, and Woolcock 2006; Grodecki 2019). However, these qualitative approaches lack specific measurement schemes for social capital, largely due to the unstructured nature of the methods.

In sum, this chapter has shown that the concepts of individual and collective social capital are closely in tune with how they are measured. Network-based individual social capital is measured by structural network characteristics, whereas multifaceted collective social capital has more associational features at the organizational level, as well as emotional bonding with generalized or unspecified others in a whole society. There is much room for improvement in the measurement of both types of social capital, using either quantitative or qualitative methods. The subsequent chapters will document and analyze how these two types of social capital have been applied in various substantive areas.

3
Social Capital, Civil Society, and Economic Development

The popularity of social capital as a concept is significant, thanks to its acclaimed association with much needed public goods in any society (e.g., Fukuyama 2001, 2002; Putnam 1993, 2000). For instance, social capital is assumed to be related to civil society (i.e., a public domain occupied by individuals and their voluntary organizations independent of the government and the economy), civic engagement (i.e., varied activities of individuals and their voluntary organizations designed to pursue public agendas), political participation, democracy, and economic development – some of which are, of course, synonymous with or strongly related to each other – these being public goods at the macro level. In short, people associate with their family, friends, neighbors, classmates, other parents at the schools their children attend, work colleagues, as well as strangers on the street in their daily lives, and those interpersonal ties may help grow a collective force to pursue various shared goals for communities and the whole society. This is an interesting transmutation of personal social relations to public resource.

It follows that the meaning of "social" that appears in the term "social capital" ranges from a microcosm of connected and unconnected ties that resides within interpersonal networks to a macrocosm of collectivities and their accompanying consciousness that may encompass an indefinite number of people and their associations. With regard to collective consciousness, it is an indispensable thread that, according to Durkheim, may weave the whole otherwise fragmented social entity together (Durkheim 1933 [1893]). It originated mainly from religion in lower societies (that is, ancient, medieval, and feudal societies) where mechanical solidarity, stemming from "elementary aggregations of quasi-familial character" (Durkheim 1933 [1893]: 91), was a governing principle of social organization. It arose from the division of labor in modern industrial societies where organic solidarity surfaced as a new principle of social organization in numerous occupations, although most occupation holders did not know one another. The use of collective consciousness or sentiment in conceptualizing collective social capital is in some sense inevitable because there is no plausible way whatsoever to measure the degree of actual connectedness among all the members of a whole social entity. Thus the socio-psychological ballpark estimate regarding the level of communal spirit among societal members – simply put, "how much do we perceive we-ness?" – needs to be used as an indicator of collective social capital. And to the extent that people of the same society share a collective consciousness, they may trust others in the belief that they subscribe to the same set of social, cultural, religious, political, and economic norms, even when the reality is that most of them are unlikely to encounter one another in their lifetimes. By this reasoning, a representative proxy indicator of collective consciousness can be generalized trust, as discussed in the previous chapter. Further, collective consciousness based on organic solidarity in the modern world may impel people to organize themselves into occupational and associational groupings so that their common goals, such as a thriving civil society or burgeoning economy, can be more efficiently realized. We will revisit this relationship between Durkheimian collective consciousness and social capital in chapter 7. In sum, I argue that collective social capital is a revived concept that reflects one of the classic sociological interests which considers how society as a moral community can maintain itself, despite the unrestricted expansion of social relations to anonymous and dissimilar others, not only within nation-states but across the globe, facilitated to a large extent by breakthroughs in information technology. And such social capital may be instrumental in pursuing collective goals.

This chapter concerns two major outcomes of social capital: civil society and economic development. Civil society was the focal concern of Robert Putnam whose ideation of social capital was conceived to explain what makes participatory democracy. This is why he stated, "Comparisons of regional governments in Italy and of state governments in the United States suggest that the quality of public administration varies with local endowments of social capital" (Putnam and Goss 2002: 6). Although in the same edited volume he mentions that associations are only one form of social capital, it is undeniable that Putnam's social capital bases itself on associationism. As such, he expresses his worry about declining social capital by showing reductions in party membership, union membership, and church attendance in OECD countries, Europe, and America between the 1940s and the 2000s. Just as collective associations are crucial to social capital, Putnam and many researchers regard trust as its key ingredient. In addition to the reductive trend in associations and associational membership across time, declining trust is implicated as the reason we are left with a weakened civil society. However, these deficiencies of associations and trust do not happen at the same rate to all members of a society. The uneven development of civil society is, Putnam argues, largely due to "the imbalances in the social distribution of social capital" because "social capital is accumulated most among those who need it least" (Putnam 2002: 415). With these multifaceted comparative schemes crossnationally and across time, the idea that social capital helps build up civil society attracted attention from both academia and the general public.

Likewise, social capital is claimed to be related to economic development, the other important outcome at the macro level. The basic argument is that the more people are connected to others and the higher the level of trust among them, then the lower the transaction costs involved in economic activity. In other words, social capital facilitates cooperation between individual and organizational actors (e.g., entrepreneurs and firms) that in turn increases the rate of contractual relations among them, with the aim of producing and trading goods and services. Thus it can be said that social capital helps enlarge economies of scale by lowering the barriers that hinder the expansion of cooperation among actors. Again, most studies in this line of research regard associations and trust as proxies of collective social capital. Interestingly, no well-defined argument has been made about the effect of declining social capital – that is, the decrease in membership in associations and level of trust in people across time – on a weakening economy and faltering development, although such an argument prevailed with regard to social capital and civil society. Instead, many studies have highlighted that a greater stock of social capital is found in economically advanced regions and countries, supporting a plausible causal relation between social capital and the economy. However, there are also some studies that deny such an association; and other studies have reported a limited association between them. Of course, we need to listen to both sides of the argument. Now we turn to the specific elements in turn: first, social capital and civil society; and second, social capital and economic development.

Social capital and civil society

Without doubt, the biggest reason that social capital has become popular is its premised relationship with civil society and grassroots democracy. According to Robert Putnam's (2000: 19) widespread tripartite definition, social capital as "connections among individuals" is made up of (1) "social networks," and (2) "the norms of reciprocity," and (3) "trustworthiness that arise from them," – in other words, the norms of reciprocity and trustworthiness originate from networks – which are in essence the backbone of any social organization, including civil society. In other words, without the three enablers of basic social exchange at the micro level, grassroots associations would be hard to form and thus their contribution to lively democracy is inconceivable. Concerning this micro-foundation of social capital, Putnam (2000: 20) also goes on to explain that "social capital has both an individual and a collective aspect – a private face and a public face ... can thus be simultaneously a 'private good' and a 'public good.'" Namely, social capital as a private good denotes personal gains from making social connections, a representative type of which, among other things, is getting better jobs, higher incomes, and promotions. This is the social capital once called social resources in the status-attainment literature in sociology (chapter 4 deals with the topic of status attainment). Further, the other social capital as a public good, Putnam argues, is made up of *externalities* (simply put, outcomes or results) unexpectedly and spontaneously yielded by selfish investments of time, money, affections in social connections that are intended to get specific returns in a tit-for-tat way. That is, unintended externalities of social connections may have spillover effects for people outside deliberately established relations which may benefit a whole community or society. In an extreme case, free-riders who invest nothing may enjoy some overflow benefits of social capital. In this regard, we may conclude roughly that Putnam's social capital as a public good is a by-product of social capital as a private good.

Theoretical reasoning: networks, trust, civil society

However, not only does Putnam rely solely on freely formed personal connections in coining social capital as a public good but he also takes voluntary organizations seriously at the meso-level which specifically aim to protect and promote public causes apart from, or possibly related to, personal gains. And thus when he tracks the historical trend of voluntary organizations such as civic associations (e.g., 4-H, Elks, Kiwanis, Lions, PTAs, Rotary, Women's Bowling Congress), nonprofit associations, national chapter-based associations, club meetings, and professional associations (e.g., American Bar Association, American Institute of Architects, American Medical Association, American Society of Mechanical Engineers), he is arguing for a collapse in American community. Specifically, Putnam maintains that social capital has decreased across time because the numbers of voluntary organizations and civic-minded volunteers have declined alongside the disappearance of a so-called "long civic generation, born roughly between 1910 and 1940" (2000: 254). So it is apparent that the idea of social capital as a public good (or collective social capital) and its major stakeholders belonging to a special generation born between the two world wars is particularly applicable to a certain nation that was militarily and economically strong enough, for example, to have participated in these wars alongside the Allies. However, the notion that social capital can help create and strengthen civil society has spread across many countries, even though many of them are not economically well developed, have lacked a tradition of civic participation and volunteerism thereof, and have distanced themselves from a participatory democracy. Anyhow, it has become a common practice to regard the number of voluntary organizations and individual membership in them as a general indicator of collective social capital. It is also undeniable that when seeking the social origins of civil society, the presence of voluntary organizations as institutionalized entities has been seen to be one of the common features of nonprofit sectors, regardless of their cultural and historical differences (Salamon and Anheier 1998). Additionally, personal networks independent of voluntary associations have sometimes been used as a measure of collective social capital.

Going back to the third component in Putnam's social capital definition above, "trustworthiness," originating in social networks, has taken another crucial position in exemplifying social capital. And it is much ingrained in cultural backgrounds because trustworthy reciprocal behaviors may be the outcome, not the source, of a culture that encourages civic and altruistic values but discourages egoistic dispositions. In such a culture, generalized social trust tends to be higher – an example of which is the neo-Tocquevillean American civil society – than in an individualistic culture (Carothers and Barndt 1999). This cultural argument has sometimes been criticized because of its obvious reference to American exceptionalism; that is, as with liberal capitalism, participatory democracy, civil society, and civic engagement are all a reflection of the American way of life. More pointedly, a civil society based largely on trust is regarded as a synonym of American morality and culture (Foley and Edwards 1998).

What is trustworthiness? Specifically, people are trustworthy when they are good at reciprocating favors, either to the givers (particular reciprocity) or indirectly to others (generalized reciprocity). A simple example of generalized reciprocity is door-holding etiquette: I hold a heavy community library door for you, expecting that you will do the same for whoever follows you. And this practice may spread throughout a community. It may sound virtuous and unselfish. But the apparently trivial practice of door holding is uncommon in many parts of the world where if you stopped for seconds to hold the door for the next person, s/he would quickly pass through without giving you any verbal or non-verbal thank you. Then you, and others who experience the same, might cease the practice, assuming that people in general cannot be trusted to return even such a minor favor. In this way, the level of trustworthiness is affected by whether and how well people in and outside of your network behave on the basis of the norms of reciprocity, be they particular or general. Therefore, it is unsurprising that the degree of attachment and enactment of the norms of reciprocity is tightly related to how moral people are. This is why Putnam mentions the golden rule – whatever you desire men to do to you, you should also do to them – when explicating trust and norms of reciprocity (2000: 135). Therefore, one may expect a high level of trust in societies that subscribe to a high degree of morality. As mentioned above, Putnam's moral analysis of the modern United States may reflect how Durkheim viewed the relationship between the industrialization of Europe and its level of collective consciousness. So Putnam checked and tracked various moral aspects of American society across time, such as the prevalence of people leading honest and moral lives, how well people observe stop signs when driving, crime rates, and employment rates in policing and the law. He argues that due to fraying trust relations, a heavy reliance on legal institutions has had to step in for numerous everyday transactions that had been informally carried out in the past, which is why the number of lawyers in the United States has grown exponentially since the 1970s (Putnam 2000: 145–7). Fukuyama (1995a) also argued for a plausible replacement of interpersonal trust with legal institutions in so-called low-trust societies, those in which people are usually unwilling to put their trust in anyone outside family or clan boundaries. These are the main reasons why the practice of signifying collective social capital by generalized trust ("most people can be trusted") in society became dominant in the relevant studies.

Empirical examination: voluntary organizations

It is not surprising that social scientists surmise that the basic features of social relations are instrumental in forming a civil society where debates, conflicts, negotiations, and collaboration with respect to public causes may occur among participants. And this process may in the end help promote a participatory democracy. I will now examine relevant empirical findings from the literature supporting the relationship. Regarding the association between collective social capital and democracy, Paxton (2002) shows using the World Values Survey (WVS) and the International Non-Governmental Organizations data that there exists a mutually reinforcing relation between social capital, indicated by generalized trust and membership in voluntary organizations, and liberal democracy across numerous countries, putting other likely causes under control such as level of industrialization, being a core or non-core country in the world system, religion, education, and ethnic homogeneity. In particular, voluntary organizations organically connected to other voluntary associations show a significant and positive relation with liberal democracy, whereas isolated organizations that "intensify inward-focused behavior, reduce exposure to new ideas, and exacerbate existing social cleavages" are negatively related to democracy (Paxton 2002: 259). Thus both trust and "connected" associations form a reciprocal relationship with democracy, confirming the democratizing role of social capital and the positive function of democracy in expanding civic associations and collective consciousness.

As Paxton suggests, not all voluntary organizations are the same in nature or may be treated equally in their relationships with civil society and democracy – suppose one mechanically counts the number of memberships in any organization, undifferentiating, for example, the Human Rights Watch and the Ku Klux Klan, and argue that it should be related to liberal democracy. This is why Knack and Keefer (1997) and Knack (2003), while examining the relationship between social capital and economy, want to make a distinction between the Putnam groups that are civically oriented toward public causes and the Olson groups that are rent-seekers, pursuing their own particular interests – the term "Olson groups" came from Mancur Olson's (1982) critical work in which he argued that special interest groups affect state policies to get more benefits for their own groups, which in the end causes systemic problems of economic inefficiency (I will revisit this issue later in the chapter). In regard to the differing roles of associations, Glanville (2004: 466) argues, "organizations are not monolithic in their influence on social network structure," and she proposes that voluntary associations may have a distinct impact on network attributes relying on organizational location and type. Specifically, she finds that associations within neighborhoods tend to increase network density, while those outside expand network diversity. Also, associations with expressive goals tend to increase network density, whereas instrumental associations help enhance network diversity. Likewise, researching six South American countries – Costa Rica, El Salvador, Guatemala, Honduras, Nicaragua, and Panama – Seligson (1999) found that among seven types of associations, including church-related organizations, school-related organizations, unions, or professional associations, only membership in community-development organizations was related to active engagement with national and local government officials to resolve public issues.

However, it has been found that the total membership count in voluntary organizations is in general positively related to civil society and democracy. This might be largely because the common survey questions about associational membership are unable to capture so-called genuine Olson organizations including, in extreme cases, hate groups; at any rate, it is not possible for various reasons (e.g., research ethics) to ask respondents if they are members of groups like the Ku Klux Klan, Blood & Honor Worldwide, or Combat 18. Supporting the general efficacy of group membership, Teorell (2003) reports that, in a social welfare regime like Sweden, even the number of passive memberships in 30 different types of voluntary association was related to political participation, after accounting for qualitative dissimilarities among groups in terms of age, gender, education, occupation, employment sectors, immigration status, and urban/rural residential status of their members. Likewise, Klesner (2007), using the 1999–2001 wave of the World Values Survey data, reports that membership in general voluntary associations is positively related to political participation, such as signing petitions, joining boycotts, or attending demonstrations, in Argentina, Chile, Mexico, and Peru. What then would be the relationship between social capital and civil society in post-communist nations? To answer this question, Letki (2009) analyzed survey data from ten East Central European countries, including Russia, Belarus, Estonia, Hungary, Poland, and Ukraine, and found that both membership in diverse voluntary associations, ranging from farmers' associations to ethnic organizations, and generalized trust were significantly related to political participation indicated by discussing politics and partisanship. Even in the existing communist state of Vietnam, total numbers of group membership were positively and significantly related to the frequency of political discussion and general interest in politics, although memberships in state-mobilized groups (e.g., unions, professional, women, and youth groups) showed a weaker association with the idea of supporting democracy (Dalton and Ong 2004). In Japan, where a hierarchical East Asian type of social relations prevails, the number of voluntary associations that people belonged to was still significantly related to political participation, ranging from voting to contacting city hall to running for elected office (Ikeda and Richey 2005).

Thus, regardless of political systemic differences and cultural variations, voluntary organizations are functional in boosting civic engagement and democracy. Under what conditions, then, do voluntary associations flourish? Schofer and Fourcade-Gourinchas (2001) ask whether certain structural contexts are more prone to engendering voluntary organizations. They propose that structure regulates action, maintaining, "Institutionalized patterns of political sovereignty and organization are associated with distinctive patterns of civic engagement" (Schofer and Fourcade-Gourinchas 2001: 807). Using the World Values Survey data from 32 countries, they found that the level of statism (power of state vis-à-vis civil society) is negatively related to the numbers of voluntary associational membership, whereas the degree of corporateness (how much a society is organized along corporate entities) is positively related to it. So they concluded that structural-cultural arrangement should be considered foremost in explaining the patterns of voluntary associational memberships. And as observed, once formed under various structural-cultural configurations, voluntary associations tend to be instrumental in making their members more civically active than non-members.

Empirical examination: trust

I now shift attention more intently to trust, another component of collective social capital, and its relationship with civil society. Most of all, is it particular or generalized trust that promotes civic engagement? Newton (1997) contrasts thick (particular) trust and thin (generalized) trust, arguing that thick trust within a small circle of people may not overflow into wider society, whereas thin trust can easily expand its range to dissimilar others encountered at the *Gesellschaft*-type of secondary associations. In turn, thin trust can promote a pluralist democracy through the cross-cutting ties it provides to diverse people which bind them loosely through organic solidarity. Concurring with this argument, Uslaner and Conley (2003) contend that those with higher levels of generalized trust (the belief that people share common values and a willingness to trust others dissimilar to themselves) would be more likely to be civically engaged in a larger society. Analyzing a *Los Angeles Times* telephone survey data set of 773 ethnic Chinese respondents in Southern California, they found, "factors associated with generalized trust foster participation in American politics, whereas attitudes and social networks associated with particularized trust lead people either to withdraw from civic life or to participate only in ethnic organizations" (p. 349). Does generalized trust then perform an effective role in growing civic engagement in mainland China too? Chen and Lu (2007) find that generalized trust had a significant and positive relationship with

Beijing residents' confidence in elected community residents' committees, support for democratic norms, and participation in the self-government system. In another study on 410 rural villages in China, generalized trust and participation in inclusive networks were found to have a positive and significant association with the responsiveness of grassroots local governance system called "villagers' committees," whereas particularized trust and participation in exclusive networks had a negative and significant relationship with it (Xia 2011). In the United States, it was also found that trust in neighbors and socializing with them was positively related to taking problem-solving actions about various neighborhood issues (Larsen et al. 2004). Lastly, with regard to Putnam's argument of declining social capital in the United States, Paxton (1999), using GSS data, asserts that it was specifically trust in individuals that declined between the mid-1970s and the mid-1990s, whereas in the same period trust in institutions and group membership did not change.

Empirical examination: personal networks

As Putnam clarified, the mainstay of social capital is personal social networks and their accompanying features, norms of reciprocity and trust. So apart from voluntary associations at the organizational level, micro-social networks need to be considered as another source of civic and political engagement. In other words, individual social capital based on interpersonal networks may also affect degrees of civicness and civility. This is what Lake and Huckfeldt (1998) wanted to know: if and how politically resourceful ties affect actual political engagement. So in a survey of 1,318 American respondents (1998: 571) they used a name generator that specifically asked "if there was someone … with whom they [respondents] discussed the events of the 1992 presidential election campaign." Also, they probed a series of questions about practical engagement in the 1992 presidential election, for instance, attending election rallies, displaying a political yard sign, bumper sticker, or campaign button, donating money to a party or candidate, or voting in the election. They found that the presence of a tie with whom one discussed the election was positively related to a higher degree of political participation and, additionally, that the larger the overall network size, the greater the likelihood of political participation, even after considering the effect of organizational belonging to up to 14 voluntary associations. Likewise, Ikeda and Richey (2005) were also interested in what informal social networks can do for political engagement. In the Japanese Election and Democracy Study 2000 survey, respondents were asked "Please recall the person with whom you talk to most (second and third most) frequently" and were further asked, "Do you talk about politics with this person?" and "Is this person a source of information about politics for you?" (p. 246). They find that informal network ties that provide political discussion and information are positively related to the level of political participation. Another study by Bian (2012) employed a position generator to identify the relationship between network social capital and environmental civic engagement, using data from the 2003 Chinese General Social Survey. He finds that network social capital is not only directly related to ten types of civic action to protect the environment (e.g., reusing plastic bags, protesting for environmental issues, or planting trees with one's own money) but also indirectly associated with it via higher environmental consciousness and a perception of environmental problems.

A plausible reciprocal impact that civic engagement may have on network expansion and increased resources has also attracted research attention. Using a position generator, Tindall, Cormier, and Diani (2012) first asked a sample of members in three civic organizations aiming to preserve wilderness in British Columbia, Canada, if they knew occupation holders of 40 jobs and, furthermore, if any of the known ties were from the environmental civic organizations to which they belonged. In turn, the level of activism was measured by an index of 17 types of actions taken, such as donating money to a wilderness preservation organization, writing a letter to a governmental agency or newspaper regarding wilderness preservation issues, or serving as a representative on a relevant advisory board. They found that the higher the level of participant activism, the greater the diversity of occupational ties developed specifically with co-environmentalists, controlling for length of membership and diversity of occupational ties in general. In line with Tindall et al.'s (2012) finding, Benton (2016) reports, using 2005 Social Capital-USA data, that civic participation measured by the number of voluntary associational memberships is significantly related to both network extensity (size) and reachability to network alters of higher status that were measured by a position generator of 22 occupations.

Dissociation between social capital and civil society?

Thus far, we have observed the public goods attributable to social capital. However, we need to be fair in evaluating what social capital can do for public goods. Is it true that social capital produces only positive outcomes for a civil society, and those externalities in turn increase social capital, forming a synergistic pattern? Is it ever possible that social capital harms civil society or even promotes authoritarian polity? A counterexample may be found in Germany. Responding to these questions, Berman (1997) asserts that it is not always true that rich social capital results in strengthened democracy. On the contrary, based on historical documents, she shows vividly how the unprecedented level of associational life in Germany in the early twentieth century debilitated the democratic Weimar Republic and promoted the rise of Nazi totalitarianism. Associations began to flourish in Germany when the new constitution adopted by the German Reich in 1871 granted universal suffrage. Numerous groups were then motivated to form associations in the hope of winning themselves a voice. Moreover, the pressure to democratize Germany after losing World War I brought a significant expansion of associational life to the nation, as a result of which, "The number of local voluntary associations grew throughout the 1920s, reaching extremely high levels as measured by both historical and comparative standards" (Berman 1997: 413). The liberal and conservative parties alike – whom people perceived as the "tools of big capitalists and financial interests" (Berman 1997: 416) – were too weak to resolve the heavy burdens of postwar economic, political, and social conflict so the Germans had to seek support from alternative civic associations. In the end, it reached a point where the general public deserted the incompetent democratic political system. According to Berman's evaluation, "What occurred in Germany was no less than an inversion of neo-Tocquevillean theory; not only did participation in civil society organizations fail to contribute to republican virtue, but it in fact subverted it" (1997: 417). As such, a political vacuum was created in the nation which Hitler and the Nazi Party astutely occupied. And the rest, including World War II and the Holocaust, is history. Satyanath, Voigtländer, and Voth (2017) support this historical review with a quantitative study of what the high level of collective social capital did to Germany. Paraphrasing Putnam's book title *Bowling Alone* as *Bowling for Fascism*, they explain how Hitler and his protégés viewed organizational building as a prerequisite for their ascendancy to power. To realize it, Nazi Party members busied themselves in formal and informal social gatherings to proselytize and win new collaborators. So the idea to be tested is whether the quantity of voluntary associations in interwar Germany was related to the expansion of Nazi Party membership. The authors collected data on 22,127 associations from 229 German towns and cities in the interwar period, based on which associational density was computed as the number of associations per thousand inhabitants. What they found was indeed that the higher the associational density in a town or a city, the greater the number of Nazi Party entries in that place. In other words, where social and civic organizations thrived, the Nazis grew at an accelerated pace. So the authors conclude, "rather than being an unambiguous force for good, our results suggest that social capital itself is neutral – a tool that can be used for both good and ill" (Satyanath et al. 2017: 520–1).

However, it is not just in Germany that we find the side effect of social capital working against participatory democracy. Civic associations in Italy and Spain also provided a conducive environment for the formation of authoritarian parties, particularly in the interwar period. Riley (2005), using the cases of Italy (1870–1926) and Spain (1876–1926), demonstrates how the strength of the associational realms in the two countries produced divergent but similar fascist political systems. Specifically, associationism in Spain was generally weaker and more regionally fragmented compared to Italy. As a result, different types of authoritarian regimes emerged in these two countries. Italy developed an ironhanded authoritarian fascist regime, whereas Spain observed a looser economic-corporate dictatorship. However, a commonality between the two was that the fascist regimes managed to infiltrate a variety of civic associations and used them as the grassroots source of their power. Thus Riley (2005: 306) concludes that civic associations "are an organizational layer of modern society that may be mobilized for various political projects," sometimes democratic and at other times authoritarian.

Newton (1997: 578) also argues that we should not assume social capital generates valuable goods and services as part of its definition, warning against the simplistic assumption that social capital is a panacea for most social ills. He also clarifies that although the orthodox Tocquevillean idea describes that social capital offers a bottom-up path to democracy, national politics may in fact determine the roles, boundaries, and limitations of social capital and civic engagement in a top-down manner, as we have observed in similar cases in Germany, Italy, and Spain. It is not that Putnam did not recognize the possibility that social capital may backfire. For instance, he mentioned that Timothy McVeigh's social capital – a strong friendship network – was a powerful source that enabled him to execute the truck bombing of the Alfred P. Murrah Federal Building in Oklahoma City in 1995 (Putnam 2000: 21). Neither this domestic terror incident nor the international terror of September 11 in 2001 would have been conducted if al-Qaeda had failed to grow bonding social capital among the terrorists involved in the four serial plane attacks. Neither would it have been possible for the US Navy SEALs to assassinate Osama bin Laden a decade later in Pakistan had they not been equipped with strong social capital among team members for a dangerous operation called Neptune Spear. Irrespective of whether the goals collectively pursued are good or evil – indeed, such ethical judgment may largely hinge on which side we take – social capital can be a double-edged sword. Thus Putnam

(2000: 350–63) also discusses this issue in a chapter on "the dark side of social capital." A focal conflict he deals with is the relationship between social capital and tolerance of racial minorities in the United States because it has often been observed that the higher the social capital within groups, the lower the level of tolerance toward out-groups. Nonetheless, he shows that the amount of overall social capital is positively and consistently correlated with the level of tolerance, racial equality, and civil liberties across the 50 states in America, and he concludes that in order to avoid the dark side of social capital, we need to develop bridging social capital that cuts across social boundaries such as race, gender, or social classes which may weaken bonding social capital within homogeneous groups. So it seems that Putnam thinks that bonding social capital is a major source of the dark side. Even though Putnam is fully cognizant of the Janus-faced nature of social capital, in the end he still accentuates its bright side.

Social capital and economic development

Rather than, or sometimes based on, the relationship between social capital and civil society, some theorists argue that social capital affects economic development. Regarding the fundamental influence of culture in the relationship between social capital, civil society, and development, Fukuyama (2001: 7) defines social capital as an "instantiated informal norm that promotes cooperation between two or more individuals" and suggests that it helps to promote associational life, a crucial precondition of modern democracy, and also to facilitate economic development by reducing transaction costs. He goes further, arguing that in developing countries that lack such an informal norm – he refers to trust mostly as an informal norm – globalization can be a source of social capital because it "is an external shock that breaks apart dysfunctional traditional and social groups and becomes the entering wedge for modernity" (Fukuyama 2001: 19). He maintains that social capital is embedded in culture, and its degree of impact on civil society and economic development is primarily contingent on what kind of culture a country subscribes ιɔ. Some researchers and practitioners have shown a great interest in this line of thought because social capital can also then be applicable to international development in terms of democratization, poverty alleviation, and economic growth. For instance, Evans (1996) regards social capital as collective efficacy that helps achieve public goods. Even when a society is impoverished, lacking material and economic resources, if its members are willing to work together in groups, economic development may be attained, due significantly to such collective efforts. This is why Fukuyama (2002) attributes the failure of the Washington Consensus in the developing world to its lack of consideration of social capital because collective capacity – including that of the state – and institutional and cultural preconditions as enablers of such capacity may be the prerequisites of successful developmental policies.

However, we need to be cautious in accepting such a causal argument because, importantly, social capital may be endogenous with development, not the cause of the latter. Social capital may be interlaced with a certain type of culture that has had a history of democracy and capitalist development, which expresses social capital as if it was the cause. So transplantation of social capital, a cultural element in an advanced economy, in developing countries is easier said than done, though not completely impossible. For instance, it was found that the relationship between social capital and the quality of government is contingent on economic development, meaning that the level of economic development not only precedes social capital but also predetermines its role (Doh 2014). Now we will see what empirical studies have reported about the relationship. Before going into detail, I should note that the empirical pattern of association between social capital and economic development is not as straightforward as has been argued.

Social capital promotes economy

Based on his study of Italy, Putnam (1993) proposes that social capital takes a positive role in economic development. For instance, regions such as Florence, Bologna, and Genoa became more prosperous than others due to the strength of the social capital they possessed. How? He reasons that networks of civic engagement fostered norms of generalized reciprocity – in other words, trust – that in turn promoted cooperation among actors. Additionally, he argues that once a collaboration experiences success in one domain, it builds connections and trust that increase the likelihood of future collaboration in other domains. He also points out that studies of rural development have shown the value of indigenous grassroots associations to be as integral as physical investment. Shifting attention to the booming economies of East Asia, he suggests, for instance, that China's economic growth after it adopted the open-door policy was more affected by *guanxi* (personal connections), which helped create and maintain contractual relations and induce investments, than it was by formal institutions.

While Putnam treats networks and trust fairly when considering their possible impact on development, Fukuyama (1995b) emphasizes the decisive role of trust in creating large-scale economic organizations in high-trust societies. Specifically, he argues that high-trust societies help economic actors widen the range of trust to unfamiliar people beyond the family, leading to the formation of large, professionally managed corporations such as Siemens, Toyota, or Ford. In contrast, low-trust societies are incapable of organizing such large economic entities because most actors in them are afraid of making commitments to non-familial outsiders. Extolling the virtues of expansive trust, he contends that social capital is "key to the success of modern societies in a global economy" (1995b: 103). Thus we may conclude that both Putnam and Fukuyama coined the cultural argument for social capital's possible relation with the economy, although in terms of degree Fukuyama's case is stronger, being close to cultural determinism.

These fundamental arguments of social capital have been put under empirical examination. First of all, Knack and Keefer (1997) considered whether social capital is related to the economic performance of 29 countries covered by the World Values Survey. Although Putnam's original study of Italy showed that economic development in its northern regions was due to their rich associational life, in Knack and Keefer's comparative study associational membership mattered for neither economic growth nor investment in those nations. Nevertheless, they find that trust and civic norms, another element of social capital, are positively related to growth in per capita income over the 1980–1992 period. Taking this a step further, they report that associational membership was unrelated to trust and civic norms, possibly because associations grew trust mostly within homogeneous groups, not in society as a whole. Instead, the degree of income equality, the strength of formal institutions, and ethnic homogeneity were positively related to trust and civic norms. Knack (2003) wanted to pinpoint the relationship between types of associational membership and economic performance, contrasting between the Olson and Putnam hypotheses. As mentioned earlier, Olson took a critical view of associations such as trade unions, professional associations, and political parties, presuming that they are selfish, putting their own interests above those of the rest of society, while Putnam favored associations like local community groups, youth clubs, cultural and sports groups, considering them a major source of network, trust, and civic engagement. He thus separated the Olson- and Putnam-types of association in the World Values Survey data and checked how overall the Olson- and Putnam-types of memberships were related to the growth of per capita income and investment (i.e., gross fixed capital formation as a share of GDP), getting the relevant information from the World Bank's World Development Indicators. Mixed results were shown. First, overall membership was not related to economic growth but associated with lower investment. Second, Putnam-type membership was negatively related to investment. Third, overall and Putnam-type membership were related to trust – note that this differs from Knack and Keefer's (1997) original study. Therefore, the Olson hypothesis was negated, whereas the Putnam hypothesis received limited support, thanks to the relationship between membership and trust.

Efforts to test the Putnam hypothesis ensued. Beugelsdijk and van Schaik (2005) examined the relationship between social capital and economic growth in 54 regions in seven European countries, including France, Italy, Germany, and the United Kingdom, using the European Values Survey data. They found that economic growth was unrelated to trust, whereas it was associated with active, not nominal, group membership. In addition, neither a Putnam- nor an Olson-type of association membership was related to economic growth. Thus Beugelsdijk and van Schaik's (2005) study runs counter to Knack and Keefer (1997) that showed trust, rather than associations, was related to economic performance. Rupasingha, Goetz, and Freshwater (2000) used county-level data from the United States to test the Putnam and Olson hypotheses. Specifically, they observed 3,040 counties in America between 1990 and 1996, looking at change in county-level per capita income as the outcome. They found that the density of associational activity – the total number of associations per 10,000 persons in 1990 – was significantly related to county-level economic performance, irrespective of whether associations were the Putnam- or Olson-type. That is, both Putnam- and Olson-type associations were positively related to per capita income in US counties. Whiteley (2000: 444), utilizing three data sources – the WVS, the Penn World Database (economic data), and the UNESCO cross-national database (educational investment) – found that trust was positively related to economic growth in 34 countries, regardless of whether they were "a democratic government or a market-based economy, since a number of authoritarian and communist countries are included in the sample." Conducting a within-country comparative study between two towns, Greenside and Shefton, near Brisbane in Australia, Woodhouse (2006) found that Greenside had a greater stock of social capital in terms of informal association, community engagement, and thin trust than did Shefton, and the former was also economically stronger than the latter. Interviews with five key informants from each town showed that businesses in Greenside were more willing to cooperate (e.g., co-organizing a Christmas lucky draw for customers), whereas such cooperation among businesses was lacking in Shefton. Hence, Woodhouse concludes that social capital seems to nurture a sustainable economy by facilitating cooperation among businesses.

Nowadays, an empirical examination of social capital and its impacts on various outcomes is increasingly carried out on data generated by online social networking services (for more details, see chapter 6). For instance, using a popular online social network service called Hyves in the Netherlands, Norbutas and Corten (2018) analyzed how regional network structures of 438 Dutch municipalities were related to their economic prosperity measured by disposable income per capita and insurance premiums at the municipal level. They find that network diversity, connecting contacts who live far away from each other, was positively related to economic prosperity, whereas network density was negatively associated with it. This study differs from earlier ones in that it takes network structural features, not trust nor associational membership, as the measures of social capital.

Social capital is unrelated to economy

It is not that most empirical studies concur that social capital promotes economic development. A significant number of studies has reported a null or sometimes a negative relationship between them. But these studies are not as much cited as those that affirm the positive relationship. First of all, Kenworthy (1997) suggests an alternative argument that claims institutional arrangements may enable the cooperative behavior of economic actors, irrespective of trust. Specifically, incentives and supports provided by states or industrial associations may affect the formation of alliances, even among competing firms in such areas as research and development, employee training, or financing. And over time these institutional arrangements may grow trust among actors. He asks how it is possible to see an increasing number of R&D alliances in the United States across time if, as Putnam argues, trust has declined. So he maintains, "trust will largely be a consequence, rather than a cause, of cooperation" (Kenworthy 1997: 649). He also measured civic engagement by voluntary association membership and voter participation, using the WVS data, and tested their relation to economic performance measures such as macro-level cooperation, firm-level cooperation, productivity growth, unemployment, and inflation, in 18 affluent countries between 1960 and 1994. In short, civic engagement was related neither to national economic performance nor to cooperation. Likewise, Schneider, Plümper, and Baumann (2000) examined whether levels of trust and political discussion were related to average yearly GDP growth rates between 1980 and 1996 in 58 regions in the European Union, using relevant data sets such as the Eurobarometer surveys. They find that levels of trust are negatively related to economic performance, while political discussion is positively related to it. Buttrick and Moran (2005) moved the focus onto post-communist Russia because it was argued that Russia's economic depression was at least partly due to lack of social capital. So they constructed a Putnam civic index in which the number of associations, newspaper readership, and voting turnout were accounted for, using regional GDP between 1994 and 2000 as the outcome measure. They find no significant relationship between the two. Thus they suspect, "social capital can be *harmful* if directed toward economically inefficient ends" (Buttrick and Moran 2005: 362, emphasis in original). Nor does another study that looked at post-communist Poland report a positive association between social capital and the economy; Działek (2014) analyzed data from 66 statistical sub-regions in Poland and found that three components of social capital (associational activity, community ties, and informal bridging capital) were unrelated to growth in personal income and of gross domestic product per capita between 2000 and 2007.

More nuanced results were reported in Casey and Christ's (2005) study on the US case. Relying on multiple data sources, such as Roper Social and Political Trends and the DDB Needham Lifestyle Survey between the 1970s and 1990s, they find no significant relationship between Putnam's social capital index (trust, volunteerism, engagement in public affairs, informal sociability) and a series of economic performance variables such as gross state product and per capita income by state. Nevertheless, they report that social capital was related to communitarian measures of economy, such as income equality and employment stability. And so they argue, "Social capital should be conceived of less as a form of capital, greater stocks of which improve economic efficiency, and more as an insurance program against instability and the vagaries of the business cycle" (Casey and Christ 2005: 843). However, Svendsen and Sørensen (2006) report that social capital measured by associational density (the total number of associations divided by the total number of inhabitants of an area) is related to neither gross income per inhabitant nor unemployment rates in 30 Danish rural municipalities. They also conducted qualitative fieldwork in those rural areas that showed most associations were prone to promoting leisure-time communities, not economic cooperation per se. Thus these studies imply that much depends on cross-national contexts; what has been found in one country may not apply to another.

So some research tried to establish whether institutional differences across countries have had a differential social capital effect on the economy. One exemplary study was carried out by Ahlerup, Olsson, and Yanagizawa (2009) who, utilizing multiple data sources (WVS, World Bank economic data, Quality of Government data from the International Country Risk Guide), examined the effect of interaction between trust and institutional quality (e.g., law and order, level of bureaucracy, anti-corruption) on economic growth (per capital GDP, investment rates). In short, they find that countries with low institutional quality benefit most from trust, a social capital measure. Specifically, they report that "a one standard deviation increase in social capital is estimated to increase growth rate by 1.8 percentage points in Nigeria, but only by 0.3 percentage points in Canada" (Ahlerup et al. 2009: 13). Nevertheless, another study shows the exact opposite trend. Peiró-Palomino and Tortosa-Ausina's (2013) comparative study of 80 countries, using five waves of the WVS data, indicates that trust did not matter for the level of income per capita in the poorest countries. Instead, the effect of trust is significant up to a certain level of development; and yet the impact of trust on the economy then decreases rapidly beyond that threshold. Again, no consistency is observed even among studies that specifically examine possible contextual effects.

Conclusion

Social capital has been acclaimed as a powerful tool to cure communal, social, political, and economic ills. The idea that the natural sociality which most, if not all, human beings possess may help resolve neighborhood problems, build a livable society, and facilitate the economy has attracted numerous researchers and practitioners across multiple disciplines and realms of activities. This chapter has dealt with the two most popular macro outcomes that social capital is presumed to be related to: civil society and economic development.

Civil society is undeniably a particular product of some Western European countries that developed both republican democracy and capitalistic industrialization as a result of which feudalistic monarchy was uprooted. And it was transplanted and recreated in America by European immigrants, the first generation of whom were the Puritans from England. The growth of civil society, some scholars argue, is organically related to the presence of civic associations and trust, the indicators of collective social capital, both of which are also more in tune with Western social organization. Thus it may be an overstretch to assume that such culturally particular collective social capital in the West must also exist in Asia, Africa, and Latin America and, further, that it promotes civil societies. Nevertheless, numerous empirical studies generally confirm a positive relationship between social capital and civil society, although the degree varies with country and region.

Nonetheless, there may be dissociation between social capital and civil society as exemplified in the cases of Nazi Germany and Fascist Italy and Spain in the early twentieth century. That is, rich associational life in these countries was abused by extremist political factions to create authoritarian regimes. In truth, then, social capital is a neutral asset that can be used to pursue either good or destructive goals – again, what is good for one community or country can be destructive for another. In short, social capital, a double-edged sword, may facilitate a totalitarian society as much as it may help constitute a civil society.

Concerning the relationship between social capital and economic development, inconsistent empirical findings have accumulated in the social science research. There are regional (within country), national, and international studies in which the relation between social capital and the economy has been affirmed; however, some studies have failed to find such a relationship; worse still, other studies have reported a negative relation between the two. Having observed all these contradictory empirical results, it is difficult to claim that social capital has a genuine effect on the economy. Criticizing the blanket endorsement of social capital's effect on economic development, Portes and Landolt (2000: 547) argue that social capital should not substitute for the provision of "credit, material infrastructure and education." In other words, social capital should not be treated as a panacea that can create the other necessary conditions of economic development any more than a 3D-printer can produce a car or a bridge instantly. The authors also warn of circular reasoning in which researchers fail to differentiate between causes and effects of social capital; any good outcome is argued to be the fruit of social capital and yet more thorough analysis reveals that the outcome was part of social capital in the first place. Significantly associated with this circular-reasoning fallacy is overgeneralization and the uncritical transference of successful cases to other scenarios. And as Portes and Landolt (2000: 537) point out, "By and large, instances of successful developmental outcomes driven by social capital have been preceded by protracted and unique historical processes requiring an evolution of years or decades." This means that, for instance, what was observed in northern Italy or in the United States is not automatically applicable to another nation with a different history, culture, and developmental trajectory.

In conclusion, this chapter has demonstrated that when the relevant hypotheses were put to empirical examination, social capital has a stronger cross-national affinity with social and political development, be it civil or uncivil, democratic or despotic, than with economic consequence. Specifically, the positive association between social capital and the economy is not universally verified. We now understand that social capital is not limited to producing public goods. It can also be effective in creating, facilitating, and executing public bads. If we perceive social capital as collective consciousness particularly fit to the historical, cultural, political, and economic composition of a society, there is no reason to believe that it must at all times be an absolute good. It can even be ugly in some cases. And this should not be surprising; just as economic capital (money) and human capital (knowledge) are sometimes accumulated and used for evil purposes, so is social capital. Nevertheless, we should not blame social capital. The blame rests with those who abuse it.

4

Social Capital and Status Attainment

In the previous chapter we saw if and how social capital relates to public goods. Collective social capital, indicated by membership in voluntary groups and generalized trust toward most people in society, often predicts, or at least tends to be associated with, public goods such as civic engagement, civil society, democracy, and, less often, economic development. However, social capital is not confined to public goods. Social capital has also been found to be in close relationship with private goods. Close and complex communal connections between parents in neighborhoods, for instance, are instrumental in lowering high-school dropout rates of their children (Coleman 1961, 1988). Also, in the world of work, those who have developed diverse ties are more likely to get job information and offers, promotions, and higher wages (Lin 1999a, 2001; Lin, Ensel, and Vaughn 1981; McDonald 2015; Son 2013; Son and Lin 2012). And this connection between social capital and personal economic payoffs has been known to persist even after some other likely factors are taken into account. The relationship between social capital and status attainment is the focal theme of this chapter, demonstrating to what extent interpersonal networks and their accompanying resources indeed produce private goods. As we will also see in the latter part of this chapter, not only individual but also collective social capital helps status attainment.

In some sense, the idea of social capital as a social resource originated in sociology, particularly couched in the 1960s and 1970s literature of social class, stratification, and intra- and intergenerational occupational mobility. I cannot here detail the entire literature on social mobility (note that chapter 1 also briefly discussed the historical lineage of social capital from the stratification literature). Yet it is pertinent to identify the particular academic tradition from which the concept came into being. It was Blau and Duncan (1967) who initiated a systematic model of social mobility, beginning with family backgrounds that may in turn affect the focal person's initial success or failure in education and occupation, which is more proximally located to the person's subsequent occupational positions some years later. The major finding of the Blau–Duncan model was that, taking both the direct and indirect effect of ascribed attributes such as family backgrounds into consideration, one's own achieved attributes were more important in predicting one's ultimately attained status. Specifically, in estimating the current status of a focal person in the labor market, the Blau–Duncan model used four predictors: parental education and occupation and ego [focal person]'s education and first job. Obviously, there can be other causes that affect social mobility than these structural factors. Thus, for instance, the Wisconsin status-attainment model developed by Sewell and Haller – the surveys administered in the state of Wisconsin to adolescents or high school seniors were often utilized, so the model name reflects it – added psychological factors such as levels of educational and occupational aspiration, influence of significant others, and mental ability (Jencks, Crouse, and Mueser 1983; Sewell, Haller, and Ohlendorf 1970; Woelfel and Haller 1971). In the midst of the booming period of social mobility literature, Granovetter (1974) introduced a proposition, the "strength of weak ties." He was mainly interested to discover what determines income in the labor market. It turned out that family background, intelligence, educational level, and occupation were not enough to predict wages. According to Granovetter, some researchers back then, becoming desperate, even mentioned that it might be luck that explains unobserved variation of income. So he tried to add another predictor: personal contacts. What he found from his empirical study of male professional-technical-managerial (PTM) workers, composed of 100 personal interviews and 182 mail surveys, was that: (1) the use of personal contacts produced better jobs for PTM workers than other formal means; (2) those workers who used weak ties (e.g., work contacts), even including some ties whose existence a job seeker almost forgot, obtained better jobs than others who relied on strong ties (e.g., family/ social contacts); and (3) non-searchers ended up with better jobs than active job searchers. Particularly related to the second point, Granovetter found that a weakly related person occupies a distinct social network from which non-redundant, valuable job information may flow toward a job seeker who cannot get such information from close contacts whose social ties mostly overlap with their own. It is around this counterintuitive finding – "weak ties are stronger than strong ties" – that a new subfield of social resources model within the social mobility literature was set up. This subfield grew into a flourishing independent research area of social capital within the sociological tradition. Specifically, this should be called individual social capital given that ties and contacts belonging to interpersonal networks are mostly the source of it. However, it should also be noted that although Granovetter initiated empirical studies of the social resources model, he treats social capital as a mere "umbrella concept" that may subsume anything under it for, he believes, the concept lacks specificity as a theory (Krippner et al. 2004: 133).

Before going into details of the relationship between social capital and status attainment, we need first to know how the social resources model was formulated within the social mobility literature. For this, we may listen to Lin's (1999a) explication. He explains that low to high socioeconomic standings are scattered around in an occupational structure of pyramidal shape, and individuals access, activate, and invest in various resources expecting returns in socioeconomic standing in the structure. That is, rational actors aim for upward mobility within structural constraints. Following Max Weber's tradition, he defines resources as valuable goods that correspond to wealth, status, and power in most societies (Lin 1999a: 467). He categorizes resources as either personal or social. This follows the ownership of resources: when an individual fully owns resources and thus can use, transfer, or dispose of them freely, they are personal resources. In contrast, when an individual does not own them but can access and activate those resources through social ties who possess them, they are called social or shared resources, in the assumption that the individual would also be obliged to lend his/her personal resources to those ties when asked. Simply put, personal resources are one's own wealth, status, and power, whereas social resources are the same properties that may be shared with and sometimes borrowed from others. As such, social resources are defined as "resources accessed in social networks" (Lin 1999a: 470). Then, concerning social resources, Lin outlines three propositions: (1) the social resources proposition stipulates that social resources help realize the outcome of an instrumental or expressive action; (2) the strength of position proposition which clarifies the original position of an actor matters in accessing better social resources; and (3) the strength of weak-ties proposition suggests weak ties lead to better social resources than strong ties, as Granovetter argues. Lin (1999a: 471) also acknowledges that other scholars in the 1980s, including Bourdieu (1986) and Coleman (1988), presented general sociological theories of social capital, each stressing a certain feature of social structure such as community norms, solidarity, or volunteerism. In contrast, he claims that social capital should refer to social resources accessed and activated through networks that may facilitate realization of the goals of instrumental and expressive actions. I call this a network-based approach to social capital.

Still, it is not personal networks and their embedded resources alone that produce status attainment. The relevant literature has also reported that voluntary organizational networks may provide social resources at the collective level that facilitate personal status attainment. So this chapter will examine how individual and collective social capitals have been associated with status-attainment outcomes. As to individual social capital, I will further divide it into accessed and activated components and relate them to social mobility. In doing so, I will review relevant empirical studies without duplicating much of what Lin has already covered in his well-cited 1999 review article.

Accessed individual social capital

The differentiation between accessed and activated social capital applies to network-based individual social capital. However, such a division may not be practically suitable for collective social capital. That is, we may know the number of memberships in voluntary associations to which a respondent belongs when a survey asks a battery of questions about group membership. However, it is rarely probed if a respondent has access to specific co-members in these associations. It is even less likely that a survey inquires whether a respondent has activated co-member ties to realize instrumental or expressive ends. In contrast, access and activation are easier to distinguish in the case of individual social capital, particularly when network generators are employed to ascertain if a respondent has access to certain attributes – i.e., names, positions, or resources – of social ties (see chapter 2 for details of network generators). And this is the reason that we are about to see if and how accessed and activated individual social capitals have been found to relate to status attainment in the relevant literature.

Accessed individual social capital indicates the volume, width or diversity, and resourcefulness of social ties that a person has accrued over time through their network. In reality, the totality of accessed individual social capital is mostly unseen and changing. Accessed individual social capital at this point in time may have increased or decreased compared with that of ten or twenty years ago. It is thus almost impossible to ascertain the exact amount, if indeed it can be expressed as a quantity, of accessed individual social capital, partly because the entry and exit of some ties in a network may not be as clear as expected to be (e.g., one person may argue, "I am your distant friend," whereas the "friend" has already expelled the former from the friendship network) and, furthermore, for various reasons a person may not be able to count all their social ties and resources. So the network generators discussed in chapter 2 were mainly to sample a tiny but representative fraction of accessed individual social capital and did not assess overall network ties and their accompanying resources.

With respect to status attainment, it has been found that accessed individual social capital is in general associated with getting a job, a promotion, a higher income, or reentering the labor market after being laid off. Mundane though this might sound, it is in fact surprising because these actors did not intentionally enlist their contacts' help in the hope of achieving outcomes which would otherwise be difficult or impossible to obtain. Instead, they just had greater accessed social capital than others, which may make a critical difference in the realization of goals. So it is sometimes called the invisible hand of social capital because it is not known how effectively accessed social capital operates to attain desired goals (Lin and Ao 2008; McDonald and Day 2010). In practice, for instance, positive outcomes may be due to unsolicited job information or offers voluntarily provided to the actors (Lee, Gerhart, Weller, and Trevor 2008; McDonald 2015). At any rate, the point is that the amount of social capital one can access may matter for status attainment even without activating it.

Erickson (2001) investigated whether accessed individual social capital is related to better jobs and higher incomes in the private security industry in Toronto, interviewing both employers and employees. Employers tended to require that applicants for upper-level managerial jobs have diverse contacts. Reflecting this need, 31 percent of the 636 job descriptions specified that applicants should have good contacts. On the employees' side, Erickson (2001: 148) reports that when a position generator was used, "People in such higher level jobs [that is, managerial positions] know someone in about 13 different lines of work on average, while supervisors and hardware workers know someone in 10, and clerical workers and guards know someone in about 9." The next question identified who got promoted to managerial jobs. It turned out that those with greater accessed individual social capital – a higher number of known positions in the position generator – were more likely to advance to upper-level jobs, after accounting for years in education and work experience, including tenure in a current job. Then, who receives a higher income? Accessed individual social capital was related to getting higher incomes. Specifically, its effect was on a par with that of education; knowing one more occupational tie added C$800 to annual income, other things being equal.

In the liberal capitalistic regime of the United States, the racial inequality in status attainment has been a serious concern, along with what accessed individual social capital may do for employees in general. Cross and Lin (2008) hypothesize that, even after accounting for prior socioeconomic status and other demographic features, (1) accessed individual social capital is related to the current status of workers, and (2) the returns of social capital may differ by race. Using the 2002 Job Search Survey data in 25 US metropolitan statistical areas, the authors found that accessed individual social capital is significantly associated with current job status indicated by occupational class, supervision, and income. However, the benefits of social capital were not enjoyed equally among racial groups. Taking the effect of social capital into account, Hispanics, for instance, registered a significantly lower current job status compared to European Americans. The authors surmise that this disparity may arise at least partly because Hispanic and African American racial minorities had about 85 percent co-ethnic ties as measured by the position-generator networks. The lack of heterogeneous ties with the racial majority group may have prevented them from advancing to better socioeconomic positions in the labor market.

Nevertheless, Son and Lin (2012) report a grimmer reality for American racial minorities. Using the identical survey data to Cross and Lin, they adopt a procedural view of status attainment, from accessed individual social capital to the activation of contacts to status attainment. Indeed, it was true that accessed cross-race ties led racial-minority job seekers to contacts with higher socioeconomic status. But those contacts mainly brought better-quality jobs to European Americans. In other words, even when racial minorities tried to draw on racially heterogeneous accessed social capital to acquire actual contacts of higher status, those contacts were prone to favor job candidates from the majority race. These racialized disadvantages of accessed and activated individual social capital have preoccupied a crucial section of the US internal labor market literature (e.g., Kmec and Trimble 2009; McDonald 2011; Royster 2003; Smith

2000). A recent experimental study by Silva (2018), relying on two-wave online surveys of the European American hiring agents, shows that when African American job applicants had the same race referrals, they were less likely to get job offers than Caucasian applicants with the same race referrals. Furthermore, African American job seekers benefited from referrals only when they had Caucasian referring employees *and* they were lucky enough to be evaluated by Caucasian hiring agents who were less racially prejudiced.

Would accessed individual social capital be efficacious in a social democratic regime where the utmost level of economic equality is institutionalized by the state? Behtoui (2007) examined the role of accessed individual social capital in the public-sector municipal services in Malmö, Sweden. A position generator of 15 occupations was used to measure the accessed individual social capital. It was found that accessed individual social capital was positively associated with educational attainment, being married, and active membership in voluntary associations, but it was negatively related to being born outside Sweden. Additionally, acquaintances (weak ties) were associated with having a greater number of accessed ties (extensity), upper reachability in terms of occupational status of ties, and range of occupational prestige as well. Finally, accessed individual social capital, a condensed factor of extensity, upper reachability, and range of occupational prestige, was positively related to belonging to the high wage group and obtaining adequate quality jobs in terms of wage level and employment security. Interestingly, whether respondents used contacts in their job search – simply put, whether they activated their social capital – was related neither to the high-wage group nor to adequate-quality jobs.

The effect of accessed individual social capital has been confirmed across countries and regions. For instance, Son (2013: 114) showed that accessed individual social capital is unequivocally related to annual income in the United States, China, and Taiwan, controlling for activated social capital and education. It is also associated with economic payoff not only for legal citizen workers but also for undocumented migrant workers. Aguilera and Massey (2003), using the Mexican Migration Project data, found that accessed individual social capital in the United States was in general related to higher hourly wages for both documented and undocumented Mexican migrant workers. However, looking closer at the ties, they identified that documented migrant workers earned 4 percent more per hour for an additional near-family tie such as a spouse, siblings, parents, and grandparents who had current or past US migration experience, whereas undocumented workers received a 1.4 percent gain for every additional far-family tie, a 4.6 percent gain for every additional friendship tie, and a 2.6 percent return for having locally embedded ties. This indicates that weaker ties were advantageous in generating higher wages for undocumented migrant workers. Next, as to the likelihood of being employed in the formal sector that in general provides better quality jobs than the informal sector, accessed individual social capital did not matter for documented workers, while it significantly helped undocumented workers to get a job in the formal sector. Therefore, social capital seems to offset the disadvantages of undocumented migrant workers.

According to the structural holes theory (Burt 1992), those who occupy a brokering position between disconnected networks tend to benefit, thanks to information asymmetry – that is, people in a disconnected network are ignorant of what happens in the other network, and vice versa, if without information from a broker who spans the structural hole between the networks. This "structural holes theory" has been impactful in the social capital literature, along with the theory of "strength of weak ties." And the two theories complement each other; the former emphasizes the merit of structural positioning between networks, while the latter highlights the unexpected advantage of having weakly related ties within a network. Additionally, the theories show how to configure advantageous access to ties within and across networks.

However, contingencies of these theories by political economy and culture have also been documented in the literature. For example, Xiao and Tsui (2007) suspect that the structural holes theory may not apply in the Chinese context where a much stronger emphasis is given to *guanxi* (private connections among actors; refer to Bian's *Guanxi: How China Works* in Polity's China Today series for a detailed explication) and in-group bonding than to the brokerage positions that do not belong to any group in particular. Specifically, they posited that occupying structural holes may be disadvantageous when collectivistic national culture is combined with a corporate milieu that requires a high level of commitment from employees. Based on quantitative and qualitative data from four high-tech industry companies in China, they found that the more structural holes appeared in a respondent's name-generator network, the significantly lower their salary and bonuses would be. The disadvantage of structural holes in terms of less economic payoff was even more serious in high-commitment companies. These results show that the structural holes theory may not be generalized to diverse cultural contexts.

As a critical response to this study, Merluzzi (2013) conducted a comparative research in which branch offices of an American firm in Asia were monitored to test the effect of network brokerage on performance. She assumed that the disadvantage of structural holes that Xiao and Tsui (2007) report was due to the lack of differentiation between national culture (i.e., collectivism) and corporate culture (i.e., emphasis on high commitment). Thus the returns to brokerage in the branch offices of an American firm deployed in Asia may reveal variation due to the interaction between constant individualistic corporate culture and differing degrees of collectivistic national cultures across countries. She categorizes regional offices in China, Korea, Thailand, Malaysia, Indonesia, Singapore, and the Philippines as belonging to collectivistic culture, while the office in Australia had an individualistic culture. Name-generator networks of about 200 employees were gathered, from which the degree of network constraint, a measure of lack of brokerage, was calculated. Performance was measured by total compensation of salary and bonus. First of all, lack of brokerage was negatively related to performance, irrespective of office location. Second, it was found that the brokerage effect applied only to top management, not lower- or middle-management staff. In conclusion, the study shows that the structural holes mattered positively for the level of employees' performance in Asian offices of an American firm, particularly at the top of the hierarchy. Nevertheless, it may not refute the impact of cross-national cultural contexts on structural holes because all the branch offices were governed by the corporate headquarters in the United States. In other words, the effect of national cultures may be more applicable to local firms to the extent that they cancel out the advantage of brokerage positions.

Does individual social capital matter in a meritocratic labor market where, in principle, only human capital and personal ability should be the determining factors in instrumental outcomes? Chua (2011) took Singapore as a contingent case to test whether accessed individual social capital measured by a name generator (i.e., knowing names of college graduates) was related to wages and preferred jobs in the state and multinational sectors. He found that accessed social capital was related to higher earnings, irrespective of job sectors, whereas actual use of job contacts, activated social capital, to get current jobs was unassociated with wages. Likewise, accessed social capital increased the probability of being employed in the state and multinational sectors compared to the less attractive small-business sector. Still, activated social capital failed to get job seekers into preferred sectors. Although the state ideology of meritocracy obscures the effect of activated social capital, it does not invalidate the effect of accessed social capital.

Briefly discussed above was the invisible hand of social capital or the effect of non-activated ties. Apart from the total volume and certain demographic features (e.g., cross-race/cross-gender ties) of accessed individual social capital, would the quality of accessed social capital make a difference to instrumental outcomes in the labor market? Cappellari and Tatsiramos (2015) responded to this question utilizing British Household Panel Survey data from 1992–2007. The survey probed respondents for information about their three closest friends, including duration of relationship, frequency of contact, and employment status. The authors defined "network quality" as having employed friends and tested its effect on the employment status and wages of the respondents. They found that network quality affected the transition from being unemployed to employed; specifically, having an additional employed friend increased the transition probability from non-employment to employment by 3.1 percentage points. Additionally, the better the network quality, particularly with non-familial close friends, the higher the wages of high-skilled workers; this did not apply to low-skilled workers.

We have thus far established that accessed individual social capital can be related to status-attainment outcomes, apart from the activation of social capital. Still, it is one thing to get access to social capital but quite another to use it for instrumental purposes. So Pena-López and Sánchez-Santos (2017: 2) argue that although accessibility to social capital may provide "an inventory of the subjects and resources," it should not be automatically assumed that the ego (the focal person in a network) can activate the accessed social capital effectively, perhaps because they lack social skills, fear not being able to return the favors, are unwilling to be indebted to others, and so forth. So it is clear that accessed and activated social capitals are organically related to each other, yet they do not completely overlap. In reality, some people who do not have any access to wanted ties seek help from total strangers, whereas others who have abundant ties shy away from activating them for instrumental goals for various aforementioned reasons. This is why we need to examine the relationship between activated social capital and status attainment separately.

Activated individual social capital

Activated individual social capital tends to be a part of accessed individual social capital that has accumulated in the labor market and outside it, such as with casual acquaintances, friends, and neighbors or through voluntary associations. In short, activated social capital is usually a subset of accessed social capital that is used for purposive action. For instance, contacts in the job-search process are examples of activated social capital. The vast majority of activated contacts in the process of status attainment are those one already knows in one way or another, although one may ask for help from complete strangers in emergency situations, which occur infrequently. So it has been a general assumption that actors rely on members of their social networks when they need assistance to achieve instrumental goals; for example, Son (2013) found that accessed individual social capital measured by a position generator was significantly related to activated individual social capital for status attainment in the United States, China, and Taiwan, an indication that activation of social capital may generally depend on how much access to it actors have in the first place.

A classic work concerning the relationship between activated social capital and status attainment is Lin, Ensel, and Vaughn's (1981) article in which the authors compare the effects of personal resources (i.e., family backgrounds and education) and activated individual social capital on getting jobs in the labor market. In short, the sampled workers in New York obtained better jobs when they activated weak ties of high status. Thus this study shows the joint efficacy of activated social capital and weak ties, reflecting Granovetter's "strength of weak ties" proposition.

Two decades later, Seibert, Kraimer, and Linden (2001) divided network structure (i.e., Granovetter's tie strength and Burt's structural holes) and social resources (Lin's), assuming that structure precedes resources. Then they looked at whether measures of social structure such as weak ties and structural holes gave access to social resources in business entities such as information, resources, and career sponsorship. They found that workers equipped with weak ties and structural holes were more likely to get contacts in other functional departments and at higher levels, which in turn brought them more information, resources, and sponsorship. In the end, this activated individual social capital within organizations produced better returns such as promotions, higher salaries, and job satisfaction for the sample of alumni who had obtained business and engineering degrees from a US mid-western university.

However, the effect of weak ties has been questioned in studies since that of Lin, Ensel, and Vaughn (1981). For instance, Murray, Rankin, and Magill (1981) could not find support for a weak-ties effect when they examined the academic job market in the United States and Canada. They found that academic job information was about seven times more likely to be provided by strong ties than by weak ties in various social science and physical science departments.

When Marsden and Hurlbert (1988) replicated Lin et al.'s (1981) study, they could not find the effect of weak ties on the measures of status attainment either. Instead, they found that particular characteristics of contact status were matched with the same characteristics of obtained status. That is, the occupational prestige of contacts was significantly related to the occupational prestige of the jobs obtained by job seekers, but not to wages, job authority, or firm size. Likewise, the industrial sectors to which the contacts belonged were significantly associated with the sectors of jobs obtained by job seekers. Another study suggested that there may be differential effects of weak ties according to the prior status of job seekers. Based on life history data for about 600 men and women in Germany, Wegener (1991) reported that job seekers of prior low job prestige tended to get better jobs through strong intimate ties, whereas those with prior high job prestige received more advantages through weak intimate ties. He was also against the idea of categorizing all ties as either weak or strong, pointing out that, "social ties between job seekers and contact persons exhibit a complex structure rather than the weak/strong dichotomy that is typically used in micromobility research" (Wegener 1991: 64).

A plausible political-economic contingency with regard to the effect of tie strength was suggested by Bian (1997). Using a sample from Tianjin, China, he found that, contrary to Granovetter's argument, strong ties (*guanxi*) functioned as trustworthy bridges in the job-search process in socialist China where high-school graduates were assigned jobs by the relevant state bureaus. Because the use of contacts was illegal, the bridging role of intermediary ties that were strongly related to both job-assigning authorities and job seekers was crucial in relieving concerns about the potential risk of punishment. In a similar vein, Bian and Ang (1997) reported that in both China (Tianjin) and Singapore, job changes were more frequently facilitated by strong ties than weak ones, attributing this to the common influence of *guanxi* culture in the two countries. Subsequently, Bian, Huang, and Zhang (2015) found that, after economic liberalization, Chinese job seekers in five large cities, including Shanghai and Guangzhou, used both weak and strong ties for different reasons – weak ties to gather informational assistance and strong ties to get favors from contacts. Favors offered by contacts had a stronger impact on getting higher-waged positions than did information. Likewise, the effect of the *guanxi* network was identified in emerging urban Chinese labor markets through in-depth interviews with workers (Huang 2008). It was shown that in state-sector companies, having influential relatives and friends was a differentiating factor when selecting employees from among numerous applicants of almost equal qualifications for entry-level jobs, although such a *guanxi* network was irrelevant when large employers in the non-state sector used a merit-based standardized hiring practice. Further, a diversity of job-search channels was found to be effective in getting better jobs: based on the 2003 CGSS (Chinese General Social Survey) data, Shen and Bian (2018) reported that Chinese job seekers who used both formal and informal job-search channels obtained positions of higher incomes than those who used either a formal or an informal channel alone. The institutional constraints of a socialist system on the use of contacts applied not only in China but also in the old European communist states. Völker and Flap (1999) found that East German job seekers tended to utilize strong ties to high-prestige contacts because they feared punishment by the state. East Germans believed a ballpark estimation that one out of every ten people in "any work group or brigade [was] an unofficial informant for the security police" (Völker and Flap 1999: 20).

Another replication of Lin et al.'s (1981) foundational study was conducted by De Graaf and Flap (1988), who compared the effect of activated individual social capital in West Germany, the Netherlands, and the United States. They found that the occupational prestige of contact status was significantly related to the occupational prestige of jobs held by Dutch respondents but not to their wages (German data did not provide measures of activated social capital). They also observed that use of informal ties was more widespread in the United States than in the other two countries and that, in general, use of informal ties led job seekers to obtain occupations of lower prestige and wages in all three countries – in other words, what mattered was the quality of activated individual social capital, not the activation of personal contacts per se.

However, with regard to the racial inequality in activated individual social capital, it turned out that minority job seekers were disadvantaged in terms of quantity of contacts, not to mention their quality. Petersen, Saporta, and Seidel (2000) looked into the ten-year cumulative data for more than 35,000 applicants to a high-technology firm in the United States where a majority of workers, specifically 68 percent of them, obtained their jobs through the referrals of friends. But only 4.9 percent of African American applicants had referrals from their friends, while 80 percent of European Americans received such referrals. Nevertheless, once applicants of minority races got referrals, they did not see disadvantages in getting a second interview and inducing salary increase between the initial and final offers. Similarly, Seidel, Polzer, and Stewart (2000) analyzed salary negotiation data of more than 3,000 job applicants for ten years at a US high-technology firm. What they found was that racial minority applicants were on average worse off in getting a salary increase by negotiation compared to others of racial majority. Still, when the racial minority applicants were referred by a friend in the hiring firm, the racial gap in salary increases was filled up. But again, the difficulty is that as Petersen, Saporta, and Seidel (2000) report, racial minority job applicants were less likely to have such a contact in the firms.

We also need to know if, how, and why the social capital of employees matters to employers. When the effect of social capital began to be recognized, the main interest in the literature was to what degree job seekers and workers realized the benefits to the job-search process, promotion, and wages. If the activated individual social capital of workers tends to get rewarded, it is logical to assume that employers want to hire workers equipped with greater social capital. That is, the demand side of employment has to be considered along with its supply side. This was the particular research interest of Fernandez, Castilla, and Moore (2000) when they looked into the employment practice of a credit card phone center at a large bank. They argue that the employers who seek to maximize their economic returns in hiring outcomes by utilizing the networks of employees are quintessential "social capitalists" (Fernandez et al. 2000: 1351). After a thorough comparison between cases of referrals by current employees and non-referrals in hiring and turnover, they find significant support for the richer pool process, meaning that referrals by current employees produce higher economic returns to the firm because the process enlarges the pool of eligible job applicants. In this regard, Fernandez, Castilla, and Moore (2000: 1290) maintain that if social capital should be called "capital" beyond a metaphor, it must present certain features of real capital such as "the value of the investment, the rates of return, and the means by which returns are realized." Then they calculate the economic returns of referral hiring in terms of savings in screening costs: the firm gave a referral bonus of US$250 as an investment, which produced a return of US$416 in the form of reduced screening costs per new hire, recording a rate of return of 66 percent.

To recap, Lin's social capital theory had two critical propositions. First, varied resources embedded in social networks may exert an independent effect on status attainment after accounting for personal resources such as family background, education, and initial achievement in the labor market. Second, weak ties are more advantageous in linking actors to contacts of higher statuses who may provide information, influence, and, sometimes, the wanted outcomes themselves. And regarding the weak tie proposition, we saw that there could be variation in the functions of tie strength by, for instance, the achieved status (e.g., occupational ranks) or ascribed status (e.g., race or gender) of actors within country and by cultural and political-economic contingencies cross-nationally. There were also critical views about the first proposition of social resources which doubt whether "who you know" does indeed help status attainment. This was the very question that Mouw (2003) examined in his empirical tests of 15 hypotheses, using four different data sets including that of the National Longitudinal Study of Youth (NLSY). In essence, he argues that a seeming causal relation between activated individual social capital and status attainment may be due to social homogeneity between actors and their contacts, meaning that it is not the effect of social capital per se but of the fact that people of similar traits tend to mingle together. Thus, he reasons, "If successful people prefer to socialize with other successful people, then this preference would result in a correlation between friends' income and occupational status even in the absence of a causal effect of social capital on labor market outcomes" (Mouw 2003: 869). In other words, once the occupational homogeneity between job seekers and their contacts were accounted for, there would be no impact from activated social capital on wages and occupational prestige. In particular, he reports using the 1970 Detroit Area Study (DAS) data which showed that when 28 percent of the same-occupation cases (that is, job seekers and contacts belonging to the same occupational categories) were dropped to eliminate occupational homogeneity, the effect of contact's job prestige on the respondent's disappeared. Hence he concludes that contacts do not matter in status attainment.

With respect to Mouw's criticism, Lin, Lee, and Ao (2013: 22) reexamined the 1970 DAS data and found that Mouw misspecified occupational homogeneity by dropping the cases where a respondent's obtained occupation and a contact's occupation were the same. This is an error because the respondent then had no time to share occupational homogeneity with the contact before s/he entered the current job. To construct a genuine test of occupational homogeneity, Mouw had to exclude pertinent cases where a respondent's *previous* occupation and a contact's occupation were the same. Likewise, McDonald (2015) found that Mouw used incorrect coding for contact users in the NLSY data. Specifically, the NLSY allowed multiple choices over 12 options in the question about job search strategies, one of which was "contact friends or relatives." In other words, respondents could choose "contact friends and relatives" as well as, for instance, "attended job training programs". However, excluding such cases, Mouw miscoded only those who chose "contact friends and relatives" as informal job seekers. McDonald also indicated that Mouw introduced selection bias in the NLSY data by employing a fixed-effects model on wages. In short, only those respondents who had multiple jobs and different levels of wages over time were allowed in the sample, omitting the rest. In conclusion, McDonald found that those who employed network-based job-finding strategy over formal job seeking had significant wage returns according to the NLSY data. Chen and Volker

(2016) used three different data sets to discover if occupational homogeneity is the determining factor in the effect of activated individual social capital. First, using the 1970 DAS data, they report that occupational homogeneity between job seekers and contacts indeed boosted the effect of contact resources. In other words, sharing the same occupational category with a contact of high status produced a job of higher prestige for a job seeker. Second, using 1992 German Democratic Republic (GDR) data which retrospectively investigated job searches during the communist period, they found that only contact resources (what level of occupational location contacts had) mattered in getting better jobs, whereas occupational homogeneity between job seekers and contacts made no difference at all. Third, using the 2002 Chinese Household Income Project Survey after the abolition of the job assignment system, the authors found that the joint effect between contact resources (Communist Party membership) and occupational homogeneity was positively related to workers' wages. Thus this study indicates that occupational homogeneity cannot eliminate the effect of contact resources. Having considered the relevant studies on the causal relationship between activated individual social capital and labor market outcomes, the key proposition of social resources in social capital theory has not been falsified, although it may be necessary to take the effect of occupational homogeneity into account.

Collective social capital

Both accessed and activated individual social capital has been found to be efficacious in producing gains in the process of status attainment. However, it is not only individual social capital that brings positive externalities for actors in the labor market. Though less frequently, collective social capital has been identified as associated with labor market outcomes, particularly in the literature of volunteerism.

As we have seen, when it comes to achieving status, a distinct advantage is realized by those who can access and mobilize the right kind of personal contacts, after accounting for the effects of family background and human capital (Burt 2000; De Graaf and Flap 1988). Individual social capital is known to be valuable because it increases the flow of information between people, provides easier access to influential others, and facilitates trust between employers and prospective employees (Aguilera 2008; Beggs and Hurlbert 1997; Lin et al. 1981; Marsden and Hurlbert 1988; Stoloff, Glanville, and Bienenstock 1999). Involvement in collective social settings that increase the range and heterogeneity of one's personal social networks – which in turn augments one's stock of social resources embedded in them – will improve one's chances of getting a higher status. Specifically, it is well known that those who hold a greater number of memberships in voluntary associations, an indicator of collective social capital, have more friends, contact their friends more frequently, and maintain more connections with people in other occupations and work organizations (Ingen and Kalmijn 2010; Isham, Kolodinsky, and Kimberly 2006; Musick and Wilson 2008; Wilson and Musick 1998).

From the point of view of employers, job-applicant involvement in voluntary associations and volunteer careers may operate as a "credential" in the hiring procedure and an "ability signaler" of desirable personality traits and dispositions, labeling those with collective social capital as suitable workers with appropriate motivation (Day and Devlin 1997). Signaling their collective social capital, job applicants indicate to hiring agencies that they will be good organizational citizens, ready to forgo their private interests for the good of the organization (Handy et al. 2010). In some sense, they are auditioning for a job with the collective social capital they possess in voluntary associations which demonstrates their work ethic, trustworthiness, and fit with the organization (Smith 2010).

Some studies have identified the actual benefits of collective social capital in status attainment. Ruiter and De Graaf (2009) found that Dutch job seekers who had memberships in voluntary associations when they entered the labor market for the first time obtained higher-status jobs and higher earnings than did non-member job seekers. On top of the benefit of membership, the intrinsic characteristics of associational members mattered too: if job seekers were members of associations that were replete with high-status co-members, they were more likely to land new jobs of high status. Wilson and Musick (2003), tracking data of a young female cohort in the US National Longitudinal Survey (NLS) in 1973–91, also discovered that the longer the women had been volunteering, the higher the occupational status they attained.

Conclusion

The main reason that I differentiate individual and collective social capitals is that they each have their dominant domains of application. Collective social capital, as we observed in chapter 3, has mostly been argued to produce *public* goods such as democracy, communal bonding, civil society, and volunteerism. On the other hand, individual social capital has displayed its strength in pursuing *private* goods in the realm of social mobility and stratification. It is thus not only that they differ in how they are conceptualized and measured but also that their purported outcomes are more akin to what they are. But, of course, these matches between the concepts and their outcomes may not be perfect as we have seen that collective social capital is related to labor market outcomes (private goods), while it is also related to public goods as discussed in chapter 3. This is understandable because individual and collective social capitals are strongly associated with each other – those who are rich in personal social networks are more likely to get involved in voluntary associations and their public activities, and vice versa – and thus their roles may not be contained within predetermined areas, producing spillover effects. As imperfect as the synchronization may be, the literature has generally shown that individual and collective social capitals have a stronger affinity with individual and collective externalities respectively.

Most of all, social resources, another name for individual social capital, appeared in the 1970s and 1980s literature of social stratification as a new predictor of status attainment. On top of other likely causes of status attainment, such as family background, education, and psychological aptitudes and traits, the resourcefulness of social networks was newly proposed to increase the likelihood of getting a better job, higher wages, and promotion. Although less differentiated at first, the division between accessed and activated social capital has become lucid as researchers sought to identify the specific roles of the sum total of social ties that people possess and the utility of particular contacts activated for instrumental purposes. Of course, it is commonsensical that in most cases access has to be established first and then activation may follow. The relevant empirical studies have generally reported that (1) both access and activation matter in status-attainment outcomes, (2) rich access without activation may still produce benefits, a pathway to which is through the provision of unsolicited job information, and (3) activation of ties has a nuanced effect depending on who activates contacts in terms of the origin status and race/ethnicity. There has been a serious question as to whether these findings do indeed indicate a causal relationship between, in particular, activated social capital and status attainment. In short, the subsequent relevant studies are in general agreement that the causality is intact, even when occupational homogeneity between job seekers and their contacts are taken into account.

Although not as frequently as individual social capital, the effect of collective social capital on status attainment has also been examined in the literature. Involvement in voluntary associations and subsequent expansion in personal networks were found to be associated with labor market utilities. As mentioned, these benefits may be a product of collective social capital because, for instance, without memberships in voluntary associations they would not be available to the actors, but at the same time they are a joint effect of collective and individual social capitals because it is also true that collective social capital enables actors to accrue greater individual social capital in collective structural settings, which may in turn directly affect status-attainment outcomes. It is notable that in regard to its relation with status attainment, collective social capital has been represented mainly by membership in voluntary associations and volunteerism. Thus trust, another major indicator of collective social capital, has not been actively put to an empirical test. For instance, Anderson and Cowan (2014: 106) report that trust is an indicator of agreeableness in terms of personality traits, and agreeableness is generally unrelated or sometimes negatively associated with status attainment. Additionally, it is also hard to locate studies that test the relationship between status attainment and norms of reciprocity, another similar indicator of collective social capital along with trust. Therefore, it remains to be seen in future research if and how psychological features of collective social capital are related to status-attainment outcomes.

To be fair, it needs to be clarified that status attainment is the most favored externality of individual social capital. And this is why the literature of "social capital and status attainment" has mostly expanded in the sociological tradition, given that stratification is one of the traditional themes of sociology. But there are other realms where both types of social capital are significantly related to outcomes of interest. For instance, health, one of the most popular research subjects in modern social science, has been found to be strongly associated with both collective and individual social capitals. And this relationship between social capital and health is what will be analyzed in chapter 5.

5

Social Capital and Health

Thus far, we have learned that social capital has roughly two versions, individual and collective social capitals, in accordance with their levels of analysis and intended outcomes. And we observed that collective social capital has a stronger affinity with various public goods (chapter 3), whereas individual social capital tends to explain more variation in personal status attainment in the labor market (chapter 4). However, it is premature to conclude that each type of social capital holds certain domain specificity so that characteristics of a particular domain predetermine which type of social capital should be utilized for certain ends. If this were true, it would render a mechanical pairing between domains of externalities and types of social capital. Yet, in reality, there exist some areas in which both types of social capital are known to contribute to outcomes of interest. One such area is health. Similar to other fields of research, studies of health incorporated social capital as a potential cause of outcomes such as physical and mental health and mortality at the personal, communal, regional, and national levels. This development has been accelerated largely thanks to interdisciplinary researchers in medical and public health schools who have been attracted to the concepts and theories of social capital since the late 1990s.

In the past, health was mostly regarded as a personal issue – being healthy or ill was a private matter. However, the advent of public health brought a new perspective that health may not be solely an individual matter and instead may be improved at the population level. This change of paradigm about how to view health, of course, involved the application of preventive interventions with the help or, sometimes, initiatives of nation-states. The public health agenda, which included the prevention of communicable diseases, hygiene, nutrition, and drug abuse, could, it was thought, be better pursued by international collaboration, which formed the background to the establishment of the World Health Organization in 1948. It was specifically in this context that some public health researchers and practitioners recognized a possibility that social capital may improve health outcomes at both individual and collective levels (Hawe and Shiell 2000). In particular, Lomas (1998) aptly describes what made social capital a necessary development in public health and epidemiology in the late 1990s. He is critical that public health and social epidemiology have not taken social environmental determinants of health seriously, emphasizing only individual interventions that may reduce the incidence of ill health. Using an example of six interventional steps for heart disease, he suggests that there should not only be personalized medical procedures, such as coronary artery bypass surgery and appropriate drugs, but also collective means of social cohesion to provide public meeting opportunities for building bonds between people. Then he clarifies that social cohesion is equivalent to Putnam's social capital – as discussed later in this chapter, this collectivistic perspective, which stresses a social cohesion approach over the network-resources approach, has been more popular in this field. Based on some evidence that the traditional public health approach of lifestyle modification programs was ineffectual, he argues that "interventions to increase social support and/or social cohesion in a community are at least as worthy of exploration as improved access or routine medical care" (Lomas 1998: 1184). Despite inconsistent ways of conceptualizing and measuring social capital in relevant studies (e.g., trust, sense of belonging, volunteering, or community participation), it has been generally agreed that social capital is significantly related to health outcomes such as self-rated health, heart disease, depression, psychological and social well-being, or even mortality (Kawachi, Subramanian, and Kim 2008).

The issue at hand now is how different types of social capital are associated with health outcomes. Specifically, the relevant disciplines such as public health, psychology, medical sociology, or social work have developed a variety of research designs where community social capital, neighborhood social capital, regional social capital, and individual social capital are empirically tested for their proposed relationship with health (Carpiano 2006; Harpham 2008). So it is necessary to divide them between collective and individual social capitals and observe how each of them has been found to be related to various health outcomes. I now examine the relationship between collective social capital and health.

Collective social capital and health

Apparently, the concept began as a spillover from the literature of social capital in political science and sociology and became popular in public health and social epidemiology. Discussing social capital in the health literature, it would be a mistake not to mention one of the early works of Ichiro Kawachi and colleagues (Kawachi, Kennedy, Lochner, and Prothrow-Stith 1997). This oft-cited article gives us a clue as to why the impact of *collective* social capital was made in the health literature before the concept of *individual* social capital landed.

Most importantly, Kawachi and his team introduced the definition of social capital as "the features of social organization, such as civic participation, norms of reciprocity, and trust in others, that facilitate cooperation for mutual benefit," quoting both Robert Putnam and James Coleman (Kawachi et al. 1997: 1491; see chapter 1 for further discussion of these theorists). Right after this introduction of the definition, he and his co-authors explained that social capital is a community-level or ecologic variable in contrast to personal networks at the individual level. Thus Kawachi and colleagues were mostly interested in social capital as a measure at the collective level. This becomes clearer by examining how Putnam defined social capital in the original work cited by Kawachi et al.: "'social capital' refers to features of social organization, such as networks, norms, and trust that facilitate coordination and cooperation for mutual benefit" (Putnam 1993). Kawachi and co-authors replace "networks" in the original definition with "civic participation." Therefore, for these authors, social networks at the individual level are separate from social capital at the collective level. The way these authors measure social capital as civic engagement and mutual trust at the state level in the United States reflects an ecologic characteristic of social capital. Specifically, they calculate the per capita number of groups and associations in which respondents from 39 states had membership (civic engagement) and the percentage of respondents in those states who disagreed that most people can be trusted and try to be fair (social [mis]trust). What Kawachi and colleagues wanted to test was whether these indicators of collective social capital play a mediating role between income inequality and mortality. They found that income inequality was negatively related to civic engagement and positively to social mistrust. In turn, civic engagement was associated with overall mortality and cause-specific mortalities such as coronary heart disease and malignant neoplasm, while levels of trust were related to overall mortality and additional cause-specific mortalities like infant mortality and cerebrovascular disease as well. After accounting for the mediatory path through social capital, the effect of income inequality on mortality greatly diminished. Making a similar argument to Putnam's declining social capital in civic America, Kawachi and his colleagues conclude, "disinvestment in social capital appears to be one of the pathways through which growing income inequality exerts its effects on population-level mortality" (Kawachi et al. 1997: 1495). They were careful to acknowledge a few possible limitations, for example, the GSS data generated representative statistics at the regional and national levels, not the state level, and the cross-sectional data did not legitimately make a definite causal argument. This article contributed to the literature of social epidemiology by introducing a new likely association between social organizational features at the collective level, called social capital, and death rates in the population. Much stress was laid on the potential efficacy of civic – not particularly interpersonal – engagement and generalized trust on health and mortality.

A year later, Kawachi and his collaborators revisited this research question in a different sociopolitical context in post-communist Russia (Kennedy, Kawachi, and Brainerd 1998). In the post-communist transitional period of about five years since 1989, Russia experienced a so-called mortality crisis in which life expectancy fell by about seven years for men and four years for women. So the authors explored whether lack of social capital was the reason for such a precipitous reduction in life expectancy. Using data from 40 of the 88 regions in Russia, they found that (1) lack of civic engagement – the share of respondents who did not vote in the parliamentary elections of December 1993 and who indicated "I am not at all interested in politics" – was positively associated with overall mortality for males and deaths from circulatory disease for both males and females, and (2) lack of trust in local government – the percentage of respondents who answered that local government was completely undeserving of trust – was related to higher mortality and lowered life expectancy for both men and women. They then surmised that, due to the lack of collective social capital, Russians in the structural transition period had to rely heavily on informal sources of support from families and close friends. But note that their measure of civic engagement was not membership in voluntary associations but voting behavior and, likewise, the indicator of trust was not generalized trust in other people but institutional trust in government. So this study does not provide a fully comparable case to the original 1997 research in the United States.

Mortality is not a sole indicator of health. So Kawachi and his colleagues employed a similar research design in their 1997 study changing the outcome to self-rated health (Kawachi, Kennedy, and Glass 1999). Data for self-rated health were taken from the Behavioral Risk Factor Surveillance System (BRFSS) which surveyed more than 150,000 persons across 39 US states. The specific item was, "Would you say that in general your health is excellent, very good, good, fair, or poor?" Then they introduced a dichotomous self-rated health variable (1 = fair or poor; 0 = excellent, very good, or good) accumulating data from the 1993 and 1994 surveys. As to the social capital indicators, data were obtained from the General Social Survey. Five years of data for more than 7,500 respondents from those 39 states between 1986 and 1990 were averaged. Specifically, they constructed state-aggregated measures of social [mis]trust, perception of reciprocity – based on an item "Would you say that most of the time people try to be helpful, or are they mostly looking out for themselves?" (Kawachi, Kennedy, and Glass 1999: 1188) – and per capita number of membership in voluntary associations. Adjusting for demographic characteristics (e.g., age, sex, and race) and individual-level variables such as income, education, health insurance coverage, obesity, and smoking, the associations between the three indicators of social capital and self-rated health remained statistically significant. In short, this study reported that collective social capital is associated with subjectively evaluated health status at the ecological level. These three studies in the late 1990s attracted subsequent research in social capital and health.

Kim, Subramanian, and Kawachi (2006) further extended the research into the relationship between social capital and self-rated health. In this new study, they differentiated between community bonding and bridging social capital and examined the associations between these two types of community social capital and self-rated health in 40 communities in the United States, using the 2000 Social Capital Community Benchmark Survey data. Specifically, community bonding social capital was measured by two indicators: first, the proportion of residents in a community who had a greater number of membership in voluntary associations than the national median and who at the same time indicated that they regarded a certain association most important along with other people of the same race, sex, and education; second, the community mean level of trust toward members of one's own racial group. On the other hand, community bridging social capital was measured by three indicators: first, the proportion of residents in a community who had a greater number of memberships in voluntary associations than the national median and who at the same time indicated that they regarded a certain association most important which was not perceived so by other people of the same race, sex, and education; second, the community mean number of times one had invited or been invited to the home of a person of a different race; and third, the community mean level of diversity of friendships. In conclusion, they found that it was community bonding social capital that was in a significantly positive relationship with health, controlling for social capital measures and other sociodemographic characteristics at the individual level. Although they suggested that they found "modest protective effects of community bonding and community bridging social capital on the health of individuals" (Kim, Subramanian, and Kawachi 2006: 122), the empirical results did not actually support the effect of community bridging social capital. Additionally, they reported that when African Americans and other races had community bonding social capital with the same race, they ended up with worse health, which hints at the partial efficacy of community bonding social capital for racial majorities. However, a similar study conducted in Japan reported that it was community bridging social capital, not bonding social capital, which was significantly related to self-rated health (Iwase et al. 2012).

Despite the causal arguments made concerning the effect of social capital on health, the studies used mostly cross-sectional data from which only patterns of association, not causality, between variables could be observed. Thus Fujiwara and Kawachi (2008a) used a sample of adult twins to control for the effects of potential confounders that may hamper causality. They sampled twins from the 1995–6 National Survey of Midlife in the United States (MIDUS) that was composed of 944 twin pairs, of whom 351 pairs were monozygotic (MZ) twins (37.2%) and 593 pairs were dizygotic (DZ) twins (62.8%). Monozygotic (or identical) twins share 100% of their genes, whereas dizygotic (or fraternal) twins share 50%. Using this disparity between the two types of twins, one may examine if an association does indeed exist between, for instance, social capital and health. Another advantage of twin samples is that each twin pair has in principle shared a living environment when they were young, such as the same parents (and equal treatment from them), household, school, and neighborhood, so that the effect of different environmental factors can be accounted for.

In this study, Fujiwara and Kawachi defined social capital as "resources accessed by individuals and groups within a social structure that facilitate cooperation, collective action, and the maintenance of norms" (2008a: 139), which is different from Kawachi et al.'s definition in 1997. In brief, there are two outstanding discrepancies: first, the later definition viewed "resources" as social capital, whereas the 1997 article claimed that "the features of social organization" are social capital; and, second, the new definition considered "individuals" as possible owners of those resources or as the level of analysis, whereas the 1997 article did not consider individuals at all in that it projected social capital at the ecological level, taking a bird's-eye view (recall that social capital existed at the US state level based on aggregated measures at the individual level). The later definition seems to be a pasticcio between Robert Putnam's and Nan Lin's theories of social capital. In addition, Fujiwara and Kawachi had another paper in which they defined social capital as "the resources that individuals access through their network," which cannot be differentiated from Nan Lin's network-based perspective (Fujiwara and Kawachi 2008b: 627) – this issue of conceptual inconsistency will be revisited in the concluding section.

Fujiwara and Kawachi proceeded to measure two types of social capital, one cognitive and the other structural. Cognitive social capital was indicated by neighborhood trust and a sense of belonging to a community, while structural social capital was assessed by the number of volunteer hours and frequency of participation in communal groups. The authors treated both self-rated physical and mental health statuses as outcomes. Utilizing a fixed-effects model, they found that neighborhood trust, a measure of cognitive social capital, was significantly associated with perceived physical health for both monozygotic and dizygotic twins, whereas structural social capital had a weaker association with health.

Changing to a different social context in Japan, Hamano, Fujisawa, Ishida, Subramanian, and Kawachi (2010) tested the relationship between social capital and mental health. They went back to the original definition of social capital that appeared in the 1997 Kawachi et al's article. A multilevel analysis was conducted in 199 neighborhoods that subsumed close to 6,000 respondents. As observed in the previous study in the United States, they found that cognitive social capital, the aggregated measure of trust of individuals living in specific neighborhoods, was significantly related to mental health, whereas structural social capital, the aggregated number of memberships in neighborhood and voluntary associations, fell short of establishing such a significant relationship. But again, this study also used cross-sectional data from which a definite causal relationship cannot be established.

Then a study in England utilized a longitudinal research scheme testing the relationship between social capital and self-rated health. Snelgrove, Pikhart, and Stafford (2009) used multi-wave data from the British Household Panel Survey to measure area-level social trust (cognitive social capital), civic participation (structural social capital), and individual self-rated health. When baseline self-rated health and other individual-level variables were fully considered, area-level social trust was associated with health; however, area-level civic participation had no effect on health. So this study reports that there may be a causal relationship between trust and health, supporting the prior cross-sectional studies conducted in other countries.

However, collective social capital has not always been found in a positive relationship with self-rated health. For instance, in Saskatchewan, Canada, Veenstra (2000) reported that neither trust (trust toward people in general, people from respondents' parts of the province, people from respondents' communities, neighbors, and trust in government) nor social participation (membership in clubs and associations, volunteering, voting, or blood donation) was related to self-rated health. Instead, income and education, indicators of socioeconomic status, were significantly related to health.

What then is the mechanism that connects collective social capital and health? Is social capital itself a cause of health or does it work through other mediating factors that link it to health? This was the question that Mohnen, Völker, Flap, and Groenewegen (2012) posed when they used three different data sets in the Netherlands to see if neighborhood social capital (contact with neighbors and friendly and sociable atmosphere in the neighborhood) affects the level of self-rated health through health-related behaviors. They found that neighborhood social capital was positively related to non-smoking and physical activity but unrelated to alcohol intake, healthy sleep patterns, and eating habits.

Both non-smoking and physical activity were associated with a higher level of self-rated health. However, when they put all of them together in a model, only physical activity turned out to be a significant mediator between social capital and health. So they suggest that neighborhood social capital promotes physical activities that in turn increase the subjective evaluation of good health. Poortinga (2006a) conducted a similar study in the United Kingdom but could not find a strong mediating role of health behaviors between social capital (trust, civic participation, and neighborhood relations) and self-rated health; however, physical activities were not considered a part of health behaviors in the study.

Carpiano (2006, 2007) approaches the relationship between neighborhood social capital and health from a different perspective stemming from Bourdieu's social capital theory (see chapter 1 for more details about Bourdieu's social capital theory). Stressing the structural conditions over cognitive features, he suggests that neighborhood social capital is a product of the structural antecedents of the area's collective socioeconomic conditions and social cohesion. These structural conditions then form a social capital that has four components: social support, social leverage, neighborhood organizations, and informal social control. As Mohnen and her colleagues (2012) depict, neighborhood social capital affects the health behaviors of an area's residents as well as their health status. Using data from Los Angeles in the United States, Carpiano (2007) reported that the increase in neighborhood social support, a form of social capital, is positively related to smoking and binge drinking. It was conjectured that living in an environment of high social support may provide more opportunities for the health-risk behaviors such as social drinking and smoking. In contrast, the more social leverage is engaged (e.g., asking advice in personal matters, participating in neighborhood organization), the less the likelihood of smoking; and similarly, the stronger the informal social control, the fewer the odds of binge drinking. As to the final outcome of health status, only informal social control was associated with perceived health. These results indicate that the relationship between social capital and health may be multifaceted and much less straightforward than had been assumed.

Is social capital related to objective outcomes of health other than self-rated mental and physical health? Aida and his colleagues (2009) raised the relevant and interesting question of whether social capital can predict the number of teeth retained in old age. The target number of teeth was 20 because the World Health Organization specified that retaining 20 functional teeth at the age of 65 years and above should be an indicator of oral health. The authors propose that there are two types of social capital, one vertical and the other horizontal. Vertical social capital is composed of groups with hierarchical relations, while horizontal social capital denotes groups with egalitarian relations – note that this division between vertical and horizontal associations was proposed in a prior study that emphasized the hierarchical nature of Japanese culture with "a clearer demarcation between social superiors (*meue*) and social inferiors (*meshita*)" (Ikeda and Richey 2005: 242). Taking a sample of more than 5,500 elderly respondents (aged 65 or older) in Aichi Prefecture, Japan, they investigated whether community vertical and horizontal social capitals are associated with the elderly having 20 or more teeth, controlling for likely confounders such as age, gender, education, income, oral health behaviors, attending a dentist regularly, smoking, self-rated health, and depression. In conclusion, they found that community horizontal social capital (e.g., membership in volunteer group, citizens' or consumer action group, sports group or club, and hobby club) was significantly related to dental health (retaining 20 or more teeth). For example, those Japanese elderly who lived in the lowest horizontal social capital areas had a 1.25 times higher odds ratio of having 19 or fewer teeth compared to some others who resided in the highest horizontal social capital communities. However, vertical social capital had no relationship with the number of teeth in the sample.

Then, using a longitudinal version of the same survey data (Aichi Gerontological Evaluation Study), Aida and another group of his colleagues (Aida et al. 2013) including Ichiro Kawachi, conducted a study where the relationship between community social capital and functional (physical or cognitive) disability (defined as difficulty in performing activities of daily living) was tested. The incidence of functional disability was followed up for four years between 2003 and 2007, recording the number of new registrations on the public long-term care insurance database. In measuring social capital, they returned to the familiar separation between cognitive (generalized trust) and structural (participation in hobby or interest group) social capitals. They then employed a multilevel survival analysis, using the discrete-time hazard model tracking the incidence of functional disability within the four-year window. The association varied by gender. That is, for elderly males, neither type of social capital at the baseline had a significant association with incidence of functional disability. However, elderly females who lived in communities with higher mistrust or lack of community cognitive social capital at the baseline had a 1.68 times greater risk of the onset of functional disability. Why females? The authors surmised that elderly Japanese females are "likely to have been more closely linked in with their communities, as well as influenced by their neighborhood social context" (Aida et al. 2013: 46). Structural social capital was not related to the onset of functional disability.

As observed, it has been documented that collective social capital measured at the neighborhood, regional, or state level is in positive association with various indicators of health. But there have recently been some critical reflections and empirical findings contradicting this unilateral argument. In short, some studies unmasked possible side effects of social capital. This is similar to the earlier social capital and civil society literature which also held a convoluted discussion describing the "dark side" of social capital.

Again, this critical discussion had to be made because of the presence of some incontrovertibly inconsistent findings. For instance, Campos-Matos, Subramanian, and Kawachi (2016) tried to expand the geographic scope of the social capital-health studies to Europe, using European Social Survey data between 2002 and 2012 which covered more than 200,000 respondents from 145 country cohorts in 35 European nations. They examined the relationship between generalized trust (cognitive social capital) and self-rated health; note that in this study they did not consider so-called structural social capital that had been typically measured by the number of memberships in voluntary associations. In regard to cognitive social capital, trust was measured at two levels: first, individual trust, and, second, contextual trust, aggregated at the country level. What they found differed from prior studies in the United States and other nations. In particular, contextual trust was unrelated to self-rated health. Instead, trust at the individual level was significantly related to health. An interesting finding surfaced when checking the cross-level interaction between individual and contextual trust. When persons who had high trust toward others lived in countries with high average levels of trust, their health status was slightly better than those with high interpersonal trust living in low-trust countries. On the other hand, low-trust individuals living in high-trust countries reported markedly worse health than low-trust persons residing in low-trust countries. In other words, the seemingly advantageous contextual condition of high-trust society does not protect low-trust individuals; instead, it can produce seriously poor self-rated health for them. The authors explain, "contexts influence different people in different ways and can even be harmful to low trust individuals, who might not benefit from other networks' social capital or produce 'bad' social capital themselves" (Campos-Matos et al. 2016: 94).

Shifting to another locale in South Africa, Adjaye-Gbewonyo, Kawachi, Subramanian, and Avendano (2018) recognized that the relationship between social capital and health cannot easily be generalized. They saw the lack of research on social capital and mental health from low- and middle-income countries (LMICs) in the literature. They also point out that many previous studies could not authoritatively establish the causal relationship between the two because they relied on cross-sectional data – simply put, surveys were conducted just once and did not return to the same respondents thereafter. For instance, Riumallo-Herl, Kawachi, and Avendano (2014) conducted a study in Chile, an LMIC, using a cross-sectional data set, and found that trust and social support, indicators of social capital, were positively related to self-reported health and negatively associated with depression. So this study employed a three-wave longitudinal data set that had more than 15,000 respondents belonging to 53 districts in South Africa, another LMIC. They measured social capital using two indicators, personalized trust (e.g., the likelihood of getting a lost wallet with money in it from someone living close by) and generalized trust (e.g., the likelihood of getting a lost wallet with money in it from a complete stranger). Mental health was reversely indicated by the number of depressive symptoms; the lower the number of symptoms, the better the mental health. Using a fixed-effects model, they found that when one had stronger generalized trust, one was likely to get a higher number of depressive symptoms, the opposite of what had been found in the majority of prior studies. Stronger personalized trust was also associated with depression, particularly in districts with low levels of personalized trust, another example of cross-level interaction. Basically, in South Africa, those who trust suffered poorer health than non-trusters. However, neither generalized trust nor personalized trust at the ecological level of districts was directly associated with mental health. The authors wrote repeatedly that these findings were unexpected. They had to suspect, "In a society with very high levels of distrust, having high trust in others, where perhaps such trust is not warranted, may, in fact, be associated with worse mental health" (Adjaye-Gbewonyo et al. 2018: 134).

The appearance of contradictory empirical findings compelled Villalonga-Olives and Kawachi (2017) to conduct a review of such studies. Examining 44 articles published since 2008, they suggest two plausible reasons why social capital is positively related to health-risk behaviors and negatively associated with self-rated health and mental health. The first they propose is social contagion, that is, not only health behaviors but also health-risk behaviors may spread throughout a group. The social capital literature has stressed the value of membership in associations as it may improve health. Nonetheless, some associations such as sports clubs and youth groups, may in fact prove a starting point for adolescents' smoking and binge-drinking careers because they encounter and may be influenced by role models who indulge in such deviant behaviors in those social contexts. So social contagion can be a source of the dark side of social capital. A second possibility may lie in the cross-level interactions between contextual social capital and personal characteristics, reported in the aforementioned study by

Campos-Matos, Subramanian, and Kawachi (2016); when low-trust individuals were situated within high-trust social milieus, their health suffered even more than those living in low-trust European societies. In addition, such cross-level interactions were identified in other studies, one carried out for 22 European nations (Poortinga 2006b) and one for the United States (Subramanian, Kim, and Kawachi 2002).

Thus far, we have observed how the epidemiologic literature of collective social capital and health took off under the influence of Robert Putnam and James Coleman. Due to the functionalistic nature of the argument ("X exists to produce Y"), the studies proposed and mainly found positive externalities of collective social capital for various health outcomes at either the ecological or the individual level. However, the relationship between collective social capital and health turned out to be not as straightforward as presumed, and the researchers realized the complicated nature of the association when they expanded the scope of the application to diverse countries and regions and tested the causal argument, using longitudinal panel data sets. In short, social capital indicated by trust was negatively associated with or unrelated to health in some studies (this was so even when Ichiro Kawachi himself tested the hypothesis in some studies). A likely reason for inconsistent associations between trust and health in the literature may be that generalized trust (that is, trust in most people), a representative indicator of collective social capital, may be misunderstood by some respondents. For example, Delhey, Newton, and Welzel (2011) report that Chinese respondents tend to misinterpret generalized trust as that held in their family and in people they know well. Thus Glanville and Story (2018) separated particularized trust in people known by actors from generalized trust in anonymous others and found that particularized trust was more strongly related to self-rated health than generalized trust in the 74 countries covered by the World Values Survey. Or another possibility is that the relationship may be reversed: that is, people with a better health status are more likely to trust others than the other way around (Giordano and Lindström 2016).

In addition, membership in voluntary associations, another component of collective social capital, was weakly related or unrelated to health outcomes (e.g., Giordano and Lindström

2011 [United Kingdom]; Giordano, Björk, Lindström 2012 [United Kingdom]; Yamaoka 2008 [Japan, Korea, Singapore, and urban China]; Yip et al. 2007 [rural China]). This may offer an explanation as to why the literature of collective social capital and health has treated trust as if it is the equivalent of collective social capital. Nonetheless, it should be noted that there are a minority of studies that report a positive association between organizational membership and health (e.g., Croezen et al. 2015 [Netherlands; the efficacy of *religious* organization in reducing depressive symptoms in the elderly]; Eriksson and Ng 2015 [Sweden; organizational membership produces better self-rated health for males than for females]; Han 2013 [Korea]; Iwase et al. 2012 [Japan]; Kim, Subramanian, and Kawachi 2006 [United States]).

Now we turn to individual social capital as a possible foundation for health. Some studies take personal trust as an indicator of individual social capital and find it generally in positive association with health outcomes (e.g., Giordano, Björk, and Lindström 2012 [United Kingdom]; Kim et al. 2012 [South Korea]; Riumallo-Herl et al. 2014 [Chile]; Yip et al. 2007 [rural China]). However, I will pay more attention to studies that employ network generators as a measure of individual social capital, maintaining the theoretical perspective that individual social capital should be network-based.

Individual social capital and health

Apart from the possible impact of collective social capital on health, can we expect that social capital composed of interpersonal relations exerts its own independent effect? More specifically, does maintaining a wider and more diverse social network have a positive effect on health outcomes? We now turn to see how individual social capital constitutes another pillar of the literature.

Ferlander (2007) criticized that, despite numerous studies in social capital and health, it is still not known which form of social capital tends to produce which particular type of health outcome. She differentiates two theoretical schools by the levels of analysis. First, the network approach pitched at the individual level is mainly interested in the gains and losses generated by access to network ties. This approach measures social capital by the amount and quality of social connections which may produce varied types of social support. Second, the communitarian (or social cohesion) approach works at the collective level, projecting social capital as a collective, not a personal, asset. The approach identifies social capital most frequently as generalized trust. As we have seen in the previous section, the social capital and health literature has been enriched by this second approach. Then she defines social capital "as a resource, individual or communal, accessed via various forms of social networks" (Ferlander 2007: 117). In particular, different forms of social capital may be produced by the direction of ties (horizontal and vertical connections), the levels of formality (formal groups vs informal personal ties), the degree of tie strength (strong vs weak ties), and the levels of diversity (bonding, bridging, and linking ties). In particular, she suggests that future studies should identify what bridging and linking social capital produces in terms of health outcomes, given that bonding social capital has been much studied. She argues that "it is vital to distinguish between these different forms of social capital, theoretically and empirically, because their impacts on health are likely to vary" (Ferlander 2007: 123). However, to my knowledge no such systematic studies that compare forms of social capital and their specific health consequences have been conducted. Instead, the majority of studies test the effect of a certain form of social capital based on the availability of data. Worse still, some studies have pursued the statistical significance of particular variables of interest on certain health outcomes, in the process of which individual and collective social capitals, formal group membership and informal ties, and horizontal and hierarchical connections are confused.

With this critical view in mind, we first need to find out what the relevant studies have reported about the relationship between network-based individual social capital and health. As discussed in chapter 2, individual social capital has usually been measured by network generators or at least some pertinent indicators of social contacts. Webber and

Huxley (2007) used a resource generator of 27 items applied to a UK sample of 335 respondents to test the relationship between individual social capital and mental disorder. The resource generator was subdivided into four internal scales: domestic resources (e.g., "Help you to move or dispose of bulky items"), expert advice (e.g., "Give you sound advice on problems at work"), personal skills (e.g., "Can repair a broken-down car"), and problem solving (e.g., "Knows how to fix problems with computers") (Webber and Huxley 2007: 486). Regarding the outcome of health, the 12-item General Health Questionnaire (GHQ) was employed: a score of 5 or higher may indicate the presence of mental disorder. The likelihood of developing a common mental disorder was associated with limited access to social resources. In other words, it may be possible that the greater the social resources accessible through personal ties, the lower the chance of having a mental disorder. Still, the authors acknowledge that this was a pilot study with too small a sample size to ascertain the reliability and validity of the social capital scales, and the response rate was too low (34 percent) to generalize the findings.

Four years later, Webber, Huxley, and Harris (2011) tackled a similar research question, using a clinical sample of depression patients in the United Kingdom. They set up a hypothesis that if patients with depression acquired access to greater resources embedded in personal networks, the social capital should help reduce their depressive symptoms. To test the hypothesis, they constructed a panel data set of two waves in six months. Specifically, the first-wave data had 173 participants. After six months, the retention rate was 91%, succeeding to re-interview 158 respondents. As to the measurement of social capital, they employed the same 27 items for the resource generator (Webber and Huxley 2007). Depression as the outcome was measured on the Hospital Anxiety and Depression Scale; the higher the score, the greater the depressive symptoms. Controlling for the baseline level of depression and other likely causes of depression, individual social capital was not related to the number of depressive symptoms after six months. In other words, this longitudinal study did not find a causal relationship between individual social capital and mental health.

Is social capital then measured by a resource generator unassociated with health? Kobayashi, Kawachi, Iwase, Suzuki, and Takao (2013) examined this question in Japan. In particular, they problematized the then status quo of the social epidemiological studies because the literature was dominated by the social cohesion approach without paying due attention to the network approach – note that Kawachi was one of the authors. They utilized the 2009 Okayama Social Capital Survey that had the 27 resource-generator items that were modeled on Webber and Huxley's (2007) study in the United Kingdom. First, they found that individual social capital captured by the resource generator was positively related to self-rated health. Second, there was a gender variation in the effects of the subscales of the resource generator. For females in particular, all four resource generator subscales (domestic resources, expert advice, personal skills, and problem-solving resources) had a clear dose-response relationship with health, meaning that the greater the resource that a female accessed in each domain, the better her health status. However, this was not the case with males; for men, only the social capital subscale of expert advice was associated with self-rated health. Why? The authors surmise that females, in particular homemakers, "spend more time in the home environment compared to men, while men spend more time in their workplaces and socialize outside work with their (mainly male) colleagues" (Kobayashi et al. 2013: 33). Therefore, women react more sensitively to all the domains of the resource generator than do men, whereas men selectively respond to certain domains such as expert advice. In addition, Kobayashi et al. (2013) argue that the resource generator should be fairer to both genders than the position generator, given that the latter does not consider non-working homemakers who do not have a formal occupation in the labor market.

Then how is social capital measured by a position generator and a name generator associated with health? Is it true that a position generator is disadvantaged in explaining health compared with a resource generator? Using nationally representative data from Taiwan, Song and Lin (2009) found that individual social capital measured by a position generator for 15 jobs was positively related to self-rated health and negatively associated with depression. However, they did not find a significant relationship between the number of ties as measured by the name generator of five close alters and health. Nevertheless, emotional social support (discussing important matters) and instrumental social support (getting help or information) offered by the ties in the name generator were strongly related to health. In addition, they identified that the impact of social support from the name generator on health was greater than that of social capital from the position generator.

In regard to the relation between individual social capital and social support, Kawachi and his colleagues earlier criticized, "By equating social capital with social networks and support, we would be simply relabeling terminology, or pouring old wine into new bottles ... The novel contribution of social capital, in our view, lies in its collective dimension" (Kawachi, Kim, Coutts, and Subramanian 2004). Verhaeghe and his colleagues (2012) investigated whether individual social capital in Belgium has an effect independent of social support, as it does in Taiwan (Song and Lin 2009). First, they measured network social capital with a position generator for 15 salient occupations in the Belgian labor market. They subcategorized social capital further into working-class social capital, intermediate-class social capital, and higher-service-class social capital. Positions occupied by acquaintances were considered to be weak ties, while positions held by friends or family were classified as strong ties. Second, perceived social support was evaluated using the Medical Outcomes Study (MOS) Social Support Scale composed of 19 items that probed "perceived emotional/informational, tangible, and affectionate support and positive interactions" (Verhaeghe et al. 2012: 360). Third, the outcome of self-reported health was assessed by asking respondents to rate their own general health from "very poor" to "excellent." The multiple regression models show that respondents with a high volume of social capital from strong ties had a higher level of self-rated health. Specifically, having family and friend ties in intermediate-class jobs was positively associated with self-rated health, whereas having them in working-class jobs proved negative to self-rated health. Next, respondents with greater perceived social support had better self-rated health.

Lastly, after accounting for the effect of social support, the impact of the total volume of social capital and intermediate-class social capital was reduced by 24 percent and 18 percent, respectively. This indicates that the effect of social capital exists independently and is mediated by social support.

Given the multiple roles of social capital that a position-generator can measure, Song (2010) suggests that it has direct, indirect, and intervening effects on health. Using a nationally representative data set from the United States, she measured social capital with a position generator for 22 jobs and depression with a shortened version of the Center for Epidemiologic Studies Depression (CES-D) Scale. First, she found that social capital was negatively related to a number of depressive symptoms (direct effect). Second, in part the social capital effect flowed through subjective social class on depression (indirect effect). Third, social capital was generated by socioeconomic status, social integration as indicated by voluntary participation and marital status, and sociodemographic features, such as age, gender, and race, and in turn affected health (intervening effect). This study shows that individual social capital is a structural product that affects health directly and indirectly.

So far, it is not clear if both individual and collective social capitals are related to health. Verhaeghe and Tampubolon (2012) examined these relations using the Taking Part Surveys of England. Individual social capital was measured by a position generator of 11 jobs and collective social capital by generalized trust. Note that meetings with friends and relatives outside the home were included as a measure of the social cohesion approach or collective social capital. But I regard it as closer to a measure of interpersonal contact. In any case, they found that both collective social capital (gener-alized trust) and individual social capital (the component score of network resources, average occupational status of resources) were related to self-rated health. In particular, knowing position holders in the salariat class (e.g., university lecturers or solicitors) produced a greater health benefit than ties in the intermediate and working classes. They also found that the effect of neighborhood deprivation on self-rated health was partly mediated by the two types of social capital. Thus this study shows that both the social cohesion and network-resources approaches may be useful in explaining self-rated health.

To confirm the association between network-based individual social capital and health, we may need objective health indicators rather than self-rated general health and depression. Moore and his colleagues (2009) checked the association between position-generator social capital and obesity as measured by waist circumference (WC) and body mass index (BMI). Using a sample from the Montreal Neighborhood Survey of Lifestyle and Health, they measured the WC using the sex-specific criterion of the World Health Organization, categorizing respondents into three groups: (1) no risk; (2) elevated risk (WCm: 94.0–101.9 cm; WCf: 80.0–87.9 cm); and (3) substantially elevated risk groups (WCm: ≥102.0 cm; WCf: ≥88.0 cm). The BMI was also divided into three groups, (1) normal (18.5–24.9 kg/m²), (2) overweight (25.0–29.9 kg/m²), and (3) obese (≥30.0 kg/m²). Individual social capital was measured by a position generator of 16 jobs. They also employed two proxy indicators of social capital: generalized trust and social participation in nine types of voluntary associations. To account for likely confounders between social capital and obesity, they also considered health behavioral factors such as physical activity, fruit and vegetable intake, and drinking and smoking. Multiple regression results showed that individual social capital from the position generator was significantly associated with no-risk WC and normal BMI. In contrast, trust and participation, the proxy indicators of social capital, were related to neither WC nor BMI. However, the authors note that, due to the small sample size (291 respondents) and the cross-sectional nature of the data, a reverse causation is possible in that obesity itself may have first resulted in smaller network resources.

Lastly, is individual social capital associated with health behaviors, the proximal conditions of health outcomes? Legh-Jones and Moore (2012) tested the association between position-generator social capital and physical activity (e.g., heavy lifting, aerobics, carrying light loads, or cycling) using the 2008 Montreal Neighborhood Networks and Healthy Aging survey. They found that both network diversity (or number of positions known, an indicator of individual social capital) and participation in voluntary associations were positively related to physical activity, whereas generalized trust was not.

Conclusion

In the early days of adopting social capital as a mechanism to explain health and mortality, public health and social epidemiologic studies favored collective social capital over individual social capital. This was mainly because these disciplines were interested in ecological social factors that may impact health and mortality at the macro level. Those studies aggregated level of trust and memberships in voluntary associations reported by individuals in the geographical divisions of neighborhood, census tract, county, city, or state to test their associations with a variety of health outcomes.

Aggregated levels of trust and social participation may be effective in describing the general social milieu within and between geographic units, but they do not indicate the degree of connectedness or disconnectedness of individuals living within them. In other words, this sort of theorization and measurement is suitable for capturing bonding social capital but incapable of analyzing bridging or linking social capital (Kawachi et al. 2004). This was why some researchers had to adopt another concept of individual social capital in health research. Conscious of this conflict between the two different conceptualizations of social capital, Kawachi and his colleagues maintain that social capital became "a contested concept" due to the "muddled usage of the term," noting that this confusion dates back to the seminal work of James Coleman, *Foundations of Social Theory* (1990), because Coleman introduced social capital as public goods but the examples he provided were of private utilities from social connections (Kawachi et al. 2004: 683). But is Coleman alone responsible for this confusion?

Although Kawachi began with the view that social capital is found in the features of social organization such as trust and civic participation rather than individual networks (Kawachi et al. 1997), he later took an eclectic position, stating, "it would be a mistake to view social capital in mutually exclusive terms, as either an individual or a collective asset; clearly, it can be both" (Kawachi 2006: 991). And, in the same year, he and his co-authors defined social capital in the opening sentence of their article, citing Nan Lin's *Social Capital* (2001), as the "resources embedded in a social structure which are accessed and/or mobilized in purposive actions" (Kim, Subramanian, and Kawachi 2006: 116). There are other cases that show the inconsistency in Kawachi's conceptualization of social capital. For instance, Kawachi, Kennedy, and Glass (1999: 1187) indicate that social capital does not include networks: "social capital measured at the community level may determine patterns of political participation and policy-setting that are more egalitarian and health-promoting, whereas social networks measured at the individual level may fail to capture these emergent group-level processes." In short, due to the lack of consistency, we do not have Kawachi's firm definition of social capital. He made the criticism that social capital suffers from a muddled usage. But he himself is not free from this criticism. In some sense, he resembles Robert Putnam in that they both preferred the collective characteristics of social capital but, when necessary, became flexible, subsuming individual networks as a component of social capital. In spite of this reasonable criticism of Kawachi, we should acknowledge his crucial contribution through his numerous academic works encompassing many countries that uncovered social capital as a key social epidemiological factor affecting population health and mortality.

As the different lengths of the two sections in this chapter show, collective social capital has been more popular than individual social capital in the academic community of public health and social epidemiology. A significant part of the reason may lie in the prejudicial citing practice of public health researchers, as Moore and his colleagues have pointed out (Moore, Shiell, Hawe, and Haines 2005). According to their citation content analysis, Robert Putnam was dominantly cited over Coleman and Bourdieu, which indicates "the hegemony of the communitarian approach" and the marginalization of the network approach (Moore et al. 2005: 1334). Their citation network analysis also showed that Kawachi and colleagues' 1997 article that introduced the communitarian (or social cohesion) approach has been heavily cited in subsequent works in public health – its network centrality score was about 17 times greater than the average. Then they suggest that the researchers should find a healthy balance between the two perspectives because, "Thinking about social capital in terms of networks ... reorients our perspectives toward the structure of social relationships and highlights the influence of nonspatial contexts on individual and population-level health" (Moore et al. 2005: 1336).

The current status quo of social capital in health research has been summarized in a glossary marking the twentieth anniversary of Kawachi and his colleagues' 1997 article (Moore and Kawachi 2017). In this piece, the authors introduce some key terms for social capital in health studies: bonding, bridging, and linking social capital, cognitive and structural social capital, negative social capital, network social capital, or social network analysis. They make it plain that there are two main approaches to social capital in public health: the (social) cohesion and the network approaches. They take a neutral position, pointing out, "While these approaches differ, they are not mutually exclusive with some researchers seeking to bridge the two approaches" (Moore and Kawachi 2017: 513).

Besides the debate between collective and individual social capitals, we need to pay special attention to the issue of causal endogeneity between social capital and health. A possible scenario is that it is likely that people who were born with good health tend to accumulate greater social capital – whichever way it is defined – across their life courses. If this is the case, it will be difficult to disentangle the intertwined correlation between social capital and health and find a clear causal direction between them. Therefore, we should be cautious about whether it is indeed social capital that affects health, which is called the argument of social causation, or whether health is a powerful determining factor that predicts the volume of social capital one obtains, which is called the argument of health selection. To tease out the genuine causality, it is desirable to use longitudinal data of high quality to determine if social capital has an independent effect on health, accounting for prior health status, family health history and genetics, relevant psychological traits, educational attainment, and other relevant sociodemographic features such as age, gender, or race. Note that a majority of the studies introduced in this chapter relied on cross-sectional data; thus it may be that we do not yet have a firm conclusion as to whether social capital is an effective predictor of health and, furthermore, whether it is collective or individual social capital, or both, that causes health outcomes. These are some of the key questions that remain to be answered by future studies in this area. In addition, many researchers have examined the relationship between social capital and subjective well-being, happiness, and life satisfaction (Bjørnskov 2003; Helliwell, Huang, and Wang 2014; Hoogerbrugge and Burger 2018; Rodríguez-Pose and Berlepsch 2014). It is desirable to distinguish the types of social capital (i.e., individual or collective) and identify if and how each type of social capital predicts well-being longitudinally and vice versa.

6
Online Social Capital

The explosive diffusion of information technology since the late twentieth century has resulted in an alternative channel of communication and socialization: cybernetworks – social relations in cyberspace (Lin 2001). Ceaseless development of internet social media (from AOL to Myspace to Facebook, Instagram, WhatsApp, Snapchat, or WeChat) and mobile devices (from Motorola DynaTAC to IBM Simon to various smartphones) has paved unprecedented ways of connecting with, maintaining, and expanding social ties across the globe in real-time communication. Therefore, the traditional concept of offline social capital may need to be modified to reflect the revolutionary change in creating social ties through cybernetworks (Ellison, Steinfield, and Lampe 2007).

Of course, it is technological breakthroughs such as internet-based social media, handheld communication devices, and relevant infrastructure including wireless communication protocols that crucially helped create online social capital. However, we should remember that social ties preexisted the advent of such information technologies. In reality, most social media platforms started from scratch with a relatively small number of participants already connected to each other. Some of them have succeeded in snowballing into a vast cybernetwork linking with total strangers from all corners of the earth who would otherwise not know of each other's existence. Nonetheless, most strangers are connected through someone who knows both parties (a "mutual friend" in Facebook). Therefore, it would have been impossible to bring a massive cybernetwork into being if there had been no prior social networks at all.

What then are the gains and losses from information technology and social media? As these are not the focal issue of the chapter, I will discuss them only briefly. As to the gains, most of all, the cost of communication has been drastically reduced as, once they are connected on the net, people nowadays make audio and video calls to each other anywhere on the globe, not to mention emails and text-messaging services which have become routine forms of communication near and far. As a result, the scale of traditional telephone and postal services has been much reduced. Similarly, there is ample opportunity to carry out economic and political activities online. It is common nowadays to find businesses that are run on internet websites and through social media, requiring minimal or no physical office space, and also that some significant part of political activity and campaigning is done online. Education is no exception; both formal and lifelong education organizations have utilized cyberspace as a venue for interactive teaching and learning, as the much-cited cases of the massive open online courses (MOOCs) and Coursera demonstrate. Medicine has seen the growth of online doctors and pharmacies as well, although concerns arise about the potential harm this may do, due largely to the lack of face-to-face interaction between patients and online medical service providers.

There can also be losses due to the advance of information technologies and social media. Robert Putnam worried about the side effects of television because he believed that the mass telecommunication medium produces couch potatoes, whose social interactions are curtailed, causing a major decline in social capital. Similarly, flourishing online social media may further deepen the trend of social isolation. It is likely that people replace costly social interactions, which require physical presence and the investment of time and money, with cheap real-time chatting and online posting of emoticons. A student mentioned in a class I taught that she became disenchanted with social media because when she informed her several hundred social media friends a few years ago that she had lost her father, comments such as "Oh, poor thing!" were the only consolation she got. Thus it is possible that the volume of online connectivity may sometimes amount to nothing of substance. On the other hand, frequent distractions in the form of social media apps embedded in mobile devices – various types of notifications calling for urgent response even for trivial matters – may hamper the level of productivity in workers and students alike. Adolescents may be impacted harder because they are more inclined to conform to peer pressure, which may in the end cause mental disturbance. Some of these issues are discussed further below.

The most important theme to consider is whether online social capital is individual or collective. I argue that it is mostly individual social capital. The reason is straightforward. As mentioned, social media on the internet utilize personal social contacts to build up their own version of a cybernetwork. The social media industry aims to expand a cybernetwork rooted in real-world social ties because the number of users determines how much is earned, mainly from onscreen advertising. For instance, Facebook claimed 2.3 billion people were active monthly users as of December 2018, based on whom it recorded a revenue of US\$55 billion in the year, principally from advertisements that users were exposed to. In some sense, the social network provided by each user is the raw material that social media companies use to create, first, their presence in cyberspace and, later, earnings. Yet those users do not get any financial return for the investment of their personal social networks in the social media firms – an unequal transaction.

For many reasons, the users of social media transfer their personal networks into cyberspace and tend to grow the size of them, partly through various technical nudges from social media platforms. Thus individual social networks form the backbone of cybernetworks and online social capital. The number of so-called friends or followers may be an approximate indicator of the extent of their online social capital, which may be supposed to go hand in hand with the volume of offline social capital. Of course, there may be some serious inflation in the number of online network ties because it is physically impossible for a human being to maintain, say, several thousand friends concurrently. (I will get back to this issue below.) In a nutshell, online social capital is a technological projection of network-based individual social capital in cyberspace.

Still, as we saw in prior chapters on civic engagement, status attainment, and health, network-based social capital can be used for various individual and collective, and instrumental and expressive purposes. Likewise, online individual social capital may not remain the informal groupings of family, friends, neighbors, and work colleagues transported to the web. Rather, it may also facilitate forming collectivities for diverse public causes. And numerous voluntary associations and nonprofit institutions have an active presence in social media. Thus, although online social capital has its roots in interpersonal networks, it can suddenly be transformed into collective social capital that sometimes involves massive civic actions, as seen in the 2017 Women's March, the 2011 Occupy Wall Street, and the 2010 Arab Spring movements.

Now we turn to a few specific themes of online social capital: first, the relationship between general internet use and social capital; second, between online social media and individual social capital; and third, between online social media and collective social capital.

General internet use and social capital

It should first be clarified whether internet use in general, rather than particular online social media, is associated with social capital and, if so, how. Before the full-scale advent of various social media channels, Wellman, Haase, Witte, and Hampton (2001) investigated whether internet use is related to social contacts, civic participation, and community commitment. Although Putnam proffered a grim view of the impact of technology on social relations, these authors argued that it is plausible that so-called couch potatoes "are going online: chatting online one-to-one; exchanging e-mail in duets or small groups; or schmoozing, ranting, and organizing in discussion groups such as listservs or newsgroups"

(Wellman et al. 2001: 437). They used data from the 2000 National Geographic Survey in which about 39,000 North Americans participated. The survey asked about activities on the internet from "send/receive email," "take part in mailing lists," "access digital libraries, newspapers, or magazines," "take online college course," to "play multiuser games" (Wellman et al. 2001: 442). Principally, they found that internet use did not increase or decrease other forms of communication with social contacts. That is, internet use did not replace face-to-face interaction or reduce the frequency of conversations over the phone. Further, internet use was positively associated with organizational and political participation. However, a negative association was found between heavy internet use and commitment to the online community. Thus Wellman and his colleagues found that general internet use does not decrease individual social capital and may increase collective social capital.

In a similar vein, Shah, Kwak, and Holbert (2001) found that internet usage types had differential associations with collective social capital. Specifically, social-recreational use of the internet was negatively associated with civic engagement (e.g., volunteering, working on community projects, and attendance in club meetings) and generalized trust ("most people are honest"). Conversely, using the internet for informational exchange had a positive association with those indicators of collective social capital. Kittilson and Dalton (2011) went further to compare the effects of online and offline social interactions on citizenship norms and political participation, using the 2005 Citizenship Involvement in Democracy survey. First, the following questions were asked in order to measure participation in virtual civil society: if the internet helped one become more involved with groups and organizations to which one already belonged; interact with people or groups who share one's political views; or interact with people from other countries.

Second, in-person social activity was indicated by the number of memberships in voluntary groups and whether a respondent actually participated in those groups' activities. As to the two outcome measures, citizenship norms were measured by political tolerance and by duty-based and engaged citizenship; and political participation was indicated by the frequency of political discussion and participation in 15 types of political activities over the past year. The authors found that both participation in virtual civil society and in-person social activity were related to citizen norms and political participation. Gil de Zúñiga, Bachmann, Hsu, and Brundidge (2013) also identified active use of the internet as being related to political participation. They differentiated consumptive blog use, which involves simply reading blogs, from expressive blog use, which requires commenting and sharing information. All things being equal, expressive blog use was associated with both offline and online political participation, whereas consumptive blog use was not. Hence, these studies show that internet use in general may have a positive impact on collective social capital.

The need to measure online social capital surfaced because of the rapid expansion of the internet. So Williams (2006) proposed the Internet Social Capital Scales (ISCS), taking Putnam's bonding and bridging social capitals into account in both online and offline contexts. In particular, there are ten items to measure bridging social capital to establish if a respondent is outward looking, has contact with a broad range of people, views himself or herself as part of a broader group, and has reciprocity with the broader community. For instance, one item reads, "Interacting with people online/ offline makes me interested in things that happen outside my town" (Williams 2006: 602). Likewise, the other ten items of bonding social capital aim to measure whether a respondent has emotional support, access to scarce or limited resources, the ability to mobilize solidarity, and out-group antagonism. An item of bonding social capital is as follows: "There are several people online/offline I trust to help solve my problems" (Williams 2006: 602). These scales have often been used in relevant studies, and we will see many of them below. However, Appel and her colleagues (2014) criticized Williams's ISCS for failing to distinguish clearly between bonding and bridging social capitals and not differentiating social capital from the similar construct of social support. These problems arise largely because the ISCS employed scale items that are "often regarded as a cause or consequence of social capital, such as social support and sense of belonging," not social capital per se (Appel et al. 2014: 408).

So they argue that the ISCS lacks validity as a measure of social capital.

In some sense, Williams's ISCS measures "perceived" bridging and bonding social capital. However, do new online contacts provide actual social resources independently from being perceived to do so? Matzat and Sadowski (2015) tackled this question using a random sample of a little short of 900 Dutch respondents in Eindhoven. They first distinguished between seven types of social media (email lists, instant messaging, multiplayer gaming, discussion forums, chat rooms, social network sites, and personal weblogs) and measured the time spent communicating with new contacts in each social medium. Then, employing a resource generator, they asked respondents if they had become acquainted with someone online over the past 12 months who had five types of actual resources, that is, knowledge, social support, access to employers, access to press or media, and physical help. Controlling for other likely confounders, they found that time spent with new contacts on instant messaging services, multiplayer games, and email lists was not related to any of those five resources. However, time spent with new contacts in chatrooms was significantly associated with social support; time spent with new contacts in discussion forums was related to social support, knowledge, and access to the press and potential employers; and time spent with new contacts on social network sites was significantly associated with access to the press, but weakly related to access to physical help. Thus acquiring new online contacts does not categorically provide access to social resources. Rather, the type of social media format one chooses may have a differential effect on access to specific resources.

These studies regarding general internet use and social capital show that the research questions we have already seen in previous chapters apply also in cyberspace. One of the focal interests was whether the new communication technology does indeed decrease civic engagement by distracting people from the public agenda, a question that had already provoked much debate with regard to the role of television. We also observed that Putnam's idea of bonding and bridging social capital offered a framework for an often-used scale of internet social capital. Critical reviews of it followed, one of which, for example, was whether the scale measures the actual exchange of social resources between persons who meet in cyberspace. We move on to the next issue regarding the relationship between specific online social media and individual social capital.

Online social media and individual social capital

The appearance of social media provided opportunities for researchers to embark on studies about whether, how, and to what extent offline social capital is transferred online. It is common that studies on social networking services rely on sampling adolescents, college students, and young adults because they are the early adopters and major users of the new communication tools.

One such study was conducted by Ellison, Steinfield, and Lampe (2007) who explored whether the intensive use of Facebook is related to the social capital of college students at Michigan State University. They suggest three types of social capital: bonding social capital and bridging social capital, adopting Williams's ISCS measures, and maintained social capital, which denotes how many high-school friend ties college students can maintain using Facebook. They found that the intensity of Facebook usage was strongly related to all three types of social capital but most strongly to bridging social capital. Additionally, students with lower levels of self-esteem and life satisfaction benefited most when they used Facebook intensely. This study thus highlighted the efficacy of Facebook usage in expanding social ties online and getting mental well-being benefit.

So do the positive effects of Facebook usage on bridging social capital and psychological well-being stand the test of time? Using a small longitudinal data set, Steinfield, Ellison, and Lampe (2008) investigated these relationships over time. Specifically, students from a Midwestern university in the United States were surveyed at two time points: in 2006, 286 undergraduate students completed the baseline survey and, in 2007, 92 of them completed the follow-up survey.

First, cross-lagged correlation analysis showed that Facebook use at time 1 was more strongly related to bridging social capital at time 2, compared to a matching lagged correlation between bridging social capital at time 1 and Facebook use at time 2. This implies that Facebook usage increases bridging social capital, not vice versa. Second, cross-lagged correlation between intensity of Facebook use and bridging social capital was higher for the low-self-esteem group than the high-self-esteem group. In other words, students with low self-esteem accessed more bridging social capital through intense use of Facebook in a year than did the other group of students with high self-esteem.

Due to the popular usage of Facebook by college students, Ellison, Vitak, Gray, and Lampe (2014) devised a new measure of Facebook-specific bridging social capital independently from general bridging social capital. For instance, modifying Williams's ISCS (2006), an item of Facebook-specific bridging social capital reads, "Through my Facebook network, I come in contact with new people all the time." They also devised a new measure of Facebook Relationship Maintenance Behaviors (FRMB), composed of a series of responsive activities to the needs or requests from Facebook friends such as "When a Facebook friend has a birthday, I try to post something on their wall" (Ellison et al. 2014: 861). Then they established that relationship maintenance behaviors were positively related to both Facebook-specific bridging social capital and offline bridging social capital. Thus it is likely that intentional behaviors to maintain reciprocal exchange with Facebook friends increase both Facebook and offline bridging social capital.

However, findings in the United States that identified a significant relationship between social networking services and bridging social capital in particular may not be generalized to other parts of the world. For instance, Choi, Kim, Sung, and Sohn (2010: 108) suspected that there were cultural divergences in the impacts of social networking services in different cultural contexts, arguing, "computer-mediated communication does not operate in a cultural vacuum." So they conducted a comparative study between US and Korean college students on the usage of social networking sites and social capital measured by the ISCS of

Williams (2006). They found that American students had a greater bridging social capital accompanied by a wider network size on average compared to their Korean counterparts. In contrast, Korean students had a significantly higher proportion of strong ties in their networks than did American students. Also, Korean respondents reported significantly higher levels of relationship development with those they meet online than American social networking service (SNS) users. Thus the relationship between SNSs and social capital may be culturally contingent; for example, in some cultures it is possible that intense usage of SNSs deepens bonding social capital.

How do the flourishing social networking sites impact the social relations of teenagers? Bearing in mind that most prior studies had college students and young adults as their target population, Ahn (2012) took a web survey sample of about 850 teenagers from two urban high-school districts in the United States to check whether Facebook and Myspace have differential associations with the social capital of teenagers. First, those who used both Facebook and Myspace had significantly higher bonding and bridging social capitals than nonusers. Second, sole membership in Myspace was related to greater bonding social capital but not to bridging social capital, whereas membership in Facebook alone was related to both bonding and bridging social capitals. The results imply that social networking sites may exert distinct effects on social capital, partly due to their unique designs and purposes. For example, Twitter has its own particular features (e.g., message length of up to 140 characters) dovetailed to fit the purpose of disseminating opinions promptly through a network of followers. According to Hofer and Aubert (2013), the time that users spend on Twitter per day was positively associated with online bridging social capital, but not with bonding social capital.

A study compared four popular social networking services in terms of bridging and bonding social capitals. Phua, Jin, and Kim (2017) postulated that subscribers to a specific SNS may have particular motives for use and gratifications derived from the service. The differential motives of use and gratification allocated to diverse SNSs, they suspected, may then lead to distinct bridging and bonding social capital outcomes.

A sample of about 300 college students from a major US university was asked to choose their most frequently used SNS among Facebook, Twitter, Instagram, and Snapchat. Then a modified version of Williams's ISCS was administered to measure bridging and bonding social capitals. They found that Twitter users had the highest mean score of bridging social capital, followed by Instagram, Facebook, and Snapchat users. The order was reversed in regard to bonding social capital: Snapchat users had the highest mean score, followed by Facebook, Instagram, and Twitter users. The authors suspect that Twitter users recorded the highest level of bridging social capital because it is a "micro-blogging platform" in which, for instance, users may follow celebrities and politicians they do not know personally (Phua, Jin, and Kim 2017: 119). On the other hand, Snapchat is a platform where users send "snaps" (photos or videos) to particular users they select. As such, the nature of interaction is private, and users send "snaps" mostly to people with whom they have already formed a close relationship.

These social networking services are mostly accessed through handheld mobile phones. So another question is whether the use of mobile phones is itself related to various outcomes that may include social capital. Related to this issue, Chan (2015) took a sample of about 500 adults aged 18–70 in Hong Kong and asked questions regarding four popular domains of mobile phone usage: (1) voice communication; (2) online chat communication, such as WeChat, Line, and WhatsApp; (3) information seeking through news websites; and (4) time-passing activities including games. The first two are communicative uses of mobile devices, whereas the latter two are non-communicative. The survey also asked questions on bonding and bridging social capitals using Williams's ISCS, and subjective well-being. They found that mobile voice and chat communications were positively associated with bonding social capital, although mobile voice communication was more strongly associated with the outcome. Likewise, both mobile voice and chat communications were positively related to bridging social capital, with the chat communication being more strongly related to the outcome. Next, mobile voice communication was significantly related to psychological well-being. In turn, when bonding and bridging social capitals entered the model, they were significantly related to psychological well-being, but their introduction rendered the effect of mobile voice communication insignificant. This indicates that the effect of mobile voice communication was fully mediated by social capital. However, mobile text communication was not related to psychological well-being. This may indicate that direct verbal communication is more relevant to mental well-being than texting. With regard to non-communicative information seeking and time-passing activities, they were not related to either type of social capital, nor to psychological well-being. The only significant association was observed between time-passing activities and negative feelings. Thus this study confirms a positive relationship among communicative activities using mobile phones, individual social capital, and subjective well-being, and it indicates that non-communicative activities conducted on mobile devices may not help increase social capital and may hamper mental health.

Chen and Li (2017) tested a similar research question, using a two-wave longitudinal sample in Hong Kong, although there was only a one-month gap between waves. They suggested three types of communicative activities using mobile phones: (1) communicative social media use (contacting known ties); (2) friending (expanding friendship ties); and (3) self-disclosure (revealing one's identity via mobile social media). They found that communicative social media use and self-disclosure were significantly associated with bonding and bridging social capital, whereas friending was not. Next, communicative use and self-disclosure were positively related to psychological well-being, but friending failed to be so. Finally, both bonding and bridging social capitals mediated the effect of communicative use and self-disclosure on psychological well-being. Thus this study suggests that communicative activity between known persons using mobile apps increases social capital which in turn brings mental health benefit. It is notable that activity that expands online friendship networks has no good outcome in Hong Kong. Another study also found that the length of time spent on WeChat by Chinese students in Germany aged between 18 and 37 was positively associated with the level of subjective well-being through both bonding and bridging social capitals (Pang 2018).

However, another study conducted in Israel fails to support findings that reported a positive association between communicative use of mobile phones and social capital. Based on a small sample of Israeli college students, Aharony (2015) examined the use of WhatsApp, a communicative messaging mobile app, to see if it is related to bridging and maintained social capital – recall that maintained social capital refers to keeping relations with previously known ties using an online networking tool. The study reports that the number of WhatsApp contacts was correlated with maintained social capital but not with bridging social capital in bivariate association. Nonetheless, the number of WhatsApp contacts was unrelated to either type of social capital when other confounders were considered in multivariate regression. This indicates that, in young Israeli adults, communicative activity using a mobile app does not widen a network any further nor does it help strengthen relationships with known contacts.

Despite the pros and cons of the effect of social media on individual social capital and mental health outcomes, many relevant studies seem to suggest that social networking sites and mobile devices are in general instrumental in keeping or expanding personal networks. As mentioned, those social networking sites utilize the personal networks of their members as raw materials to process in one way or another. In the end, they earn income mostly from advertisements based on the number of subscribers or, in other words, based on their cybernetwork size. So this is an indirect way of profiteering from personal social networks (Faucher 2018). However, this also indicates that numerous firms sell their products directly through online social media, which is called e-commerce. Hensel and Deis (2010) emphasize that social media enable e-commerce companies to get immediate feedback from customers and hence they can promptly address pertinent issues. Furthermore, customers may also be involved in the innovation process, potentially lowering research and development costs for the companies. Additionally, companies may obtain data through online commerce about the profile of customers, such as their "age, gender, zip code, money spent, material purchases, and other details of information relevant to the market content that is desired" (Hensel and Deis 2010: 93).

Under unpredictable market situations, cost effectiveness is one of the crucial factors that increases the portion of e-commerce compared to the traditional ways of approaching customers via mass media such as television, newspapers, and magazines. In particular, the dependence on social media became heavier after the global economic crisis in 2008 because they were a cheaper but more effective alternative than traditional mass media. According to Kirtis and Karahan (2011: 264), 84 firms among the global Fortune 100 companies in 2011 utilized at least one of four forms of social media platforms, viz. Twitter, Facebook, YouTube, and corporate blog applications, and 25 of them used all four. For both small and large firms, cost can be much reduced due to the fact that access to most social media is in principle free.

Once the relevant advertisements and information about products hit customers through social media, it may not be the end of the marketing process but a beginning of its further spread over informal networks, which is out of the companies' control. Hence, Pinho and Soares (2015) checked the relationship between online social capital, sociability, social status, and response to advertising, using a small sample of nearly 300 social media users. They found that bridging social capital is related to both social status and sociability that in turn increase the responsiveness to advertising. In other words, online social capital, resources embedded in online social networks, affects the success or failure of marketing efforts because "users are likely to click on advertisements, to pay attention and search for related information about advertisements shown by their online social friends, particularly by those who evidence higher social status and sociability" (Pinho and Soares 2015: 246).

As we have observed, online social media has an inseparable relation with individual social capital. Without the presence of individual social capital, it is impossible or even meaningless to construct a cybernetwork through social networking services. Nevertheless, it is also true that online social media can affect individual social capital, whether it be bonding, bridging, or maintained. And online social media may indirectly affect mental health through its effect on individual social capital as we read in chapter 5 regarding the relationship between social capital and health. In addition, online social media provide a viable marketing channel for companies, a practical example of the social embeddedness of economic activities (Granovetter 1985).

Online social media and collective social capital

Compared with the previous section, fewer studies have examined the relationship between online social media and collective social capital. This is mainly because the cyber-networks that online social media have constructed are largely a virtual projection of individual social capital. Still, it is naturally of research interest to identify if social media are associated with civic engagement, volunteerism, and generalized trust, indicators of collective social capital. Most studies generally supported a positive association between social media and collective social capital, although there were some contingencies that moderated the degree.

Valenzuela, Park, and Kee (2009) hypothesized that Facebook users may increase their chance of civic engagement due to the News Feed and Facebook Groups functions because these can help strengthen personal ties by updating events to Facebook friends, forming online groups following common interests among like-minded users, and mobilizing people to act on collective causes in various online and offline ways. In addition, they postulated that Facebook usage may solidify norms of reciprocity and trust. Using a large sample of about 2,600 college students in Texas, United States, they asked a series of questions about civic and political participation, including volunteering for community projects and non-political or political groups, fundraising for charity, voting in local and national elections, signing petitions, wearing badges for a political or social cause, or purchasing particular products for political, ethical, or environmental reasons (Valenzuela, Park, and Kee 2009: 885). They found through multivariate regressions that both the intensity of Facebook use and Facebook group use were significantly related to civic participation, while only the intensity of Facebook group use was associated with political participation. They further checked if the type of Facebook group had a significant relationship with political participation. It turned out that being a member of a political Facebook group or a student Facebook group was significantly related to political participation. In addition, the intensity of Facebook use was related to generalized trust. The authors conclude that it is wrong to assume that Facebook categorically disengages young adults from the civic domain. Nonetheless, they declare a caveat that the association between variables related to Facebook and civic engagement were small, suggesting that Facebook, or social media in general, may provide only an auxiliary path to civic engagement. In another study, Gil de Zúñiga, Jung, and Valenzuela (2012) also found that the use of social networking sites for news in the United States was related to social capital and civic participation and to on- and offline political participation. Furthermore, Gil de Zúñiga, Barnidge, and Scherman (2017) argue not only that social media social capital generated by social networking sites is distinct from offline social capital but also that it produces a higher level of political participation than offline social capital. Using a two-wave panel survey sample of about a thousand respondents in the United States, they report that social media social capital was positively related to both online and offline political participation, whereas offline social capital was not associated with offline political participation. So this study concludes that online social capital is a more effective source of political participation.

However, there may be some moderation of the relationship between online social media and civic engagement by political and cultural contingencies. Zhong's (2014) study took a sample of about 650 college students in Guangzhou, China, and tested to see if there is a robust relationship among SNS use, online and offline social capital, and online and offline civic engagement. First, using SNS to meet new people was related only to online social capital, whereas using SNS to meet friends was associated only with offline social capital. Second, in turn, online social capital was related only to online civic engagement, but offline social capital only to offline civic engagement. In other words, Chinese college students conduct offline civic engagement with their friends and offline social capital attached to them, but they do not rely on new people they meet online. Similarly, Skoric, Ying, and Ng (2009) found that, from a sample of about 360 internet users aged 18 years or older in Singapore, although online bridging social capital was significantly related to online political participation, it was unrelated to offline political participation. Instead, only online bonding social capital was associated with traditional political participation. It was surmised, "strong online bonding ties may alleviate the fears associated with attending political rallies, speaking publicly about politics or joining political parties, which certainly represent barriers to traditional political participation in Singapore" (Skoric, Ying, and Ng 2009: 427). Hence, in countries where civic engagement and political participation are controlled by the state, online social capital may have limited or even no effect on them because actors cannot easily trust persons they encounter on the internet and in social media without prior face-to-face interaction.

Interestingly, studies on online gaming are usually about collective social capital. This may be due to online gaming being a virtual group activity, albeit one in which gamers may join from all over the world. Regarding the impact of online gaming on forming social relations, Skoric and Kwan (2011) suggest that massively multiplayer online games (MMOs) function as a communication medium between the players. And they found, using a sample of Singaporean young adults aged between 18 and 29 years, that the civic type of MMO – multiplayer online games with civic, moral, and ethical issues – was related to online bridging social capital, whereas the non-civic type of MMO was associated with online bonding social capital, which indicates that the multiplayer gaming experience may help form ties with new players and increase the relational depth among co-players.

Then does online gaming affect social capital and civic engagement? Zhong (2011: 2352) selected massively multiplayer online role-playing games (MMORPGs) that enable "hundreds or thousands of geographically distributed players to simultaneously play on the internet" and examined their association with social capital and civic engagement. In these games, participants assume fictional characters called avatars, interact with other players, join virtual communities, and cooperate with them to fulfill certain tasks. Notably, the quests in MMORPGs are often hard to complete alone, so players join guilds. These cooperative associations and activities may form social capital in an online gaming context. About 230 Chinese gamers completed two waves of the survey, which allows a cross-lagged model whereby temporal causal relations can be tested. Other things being equal, it turned out that collective play at the first wave – measured by frequency of guild actions in a week and a gamer's, a leader's, and other members' evaluations of the guild – was directly related to offline civic engagement at the second wave, while the length of gaming time was negatively related to it. In addition, collective play was also associated with online civic engagement and online bonding and bridging social capitals. However, collective play did not affect offline bonding and bridging social capitals, possibly because some dedicated gamers regard co-players in MMORPGs to be more important than offline contacts. In short, the experience of collective play in MMORPGs may help enhance offline civic engagement.

Kobayashi (2010) asked if network heterogeneity in terms of age, gender, occupation, residential area, or lifestyle among gamers of *Lineage*, a MMORPG, results in a higher level of social tolerance toward people who have different traits. Using three-wave panel data for Japanese gamers, the study found that network heterogeneity in the online gaming community promotes interpersonal social tolerance toward other online members that in turn increases interpersonal social tolerance offline. In a similar vein, Lundmark (2015) tested the effect of collective gaming on generalized trust among gamers in *World of Warcraft* (WoW), another MMORPG. Relying on a three-wave panel study of about 530 gamers, the study found that guild membership was positively associated with generalized trust, whereas exit from it decreased the degree of trust. So he concludes, "gaming together in voluntary association-like environments online might actually be a good response to the proposed negative effect of bowling alone" (Lundmark 2015: 65).

Emphasizing the positive role of multiplayer video gaming, Molyneux, Vasudevan, and Gil de Zúñiga (2015: 382) proposed that gaming social capital – defined as "one's sense of belonging to and participating in a gaming community" – increases offline individual social capital and civic engagement. Based on a nationally representative sample of American adults, they find that (1) multiplayer gaming is the strongest predictor of gaming social capital, (2) gaming social capital is positively related to both offline social capital and civic engagement, and (3) offline social capital is also significantly associated with civic engagement. Hence this study proposes that gaming social capital causes offline social capital, not the other way around, and also affects civic engagement independently of the effect of offline social capital. It is plausible that online social media and multiplayer gaming have an independent effect on social relations. However, it would be rash to conclude that separate conceptual entities such as social media social capital and gaming social capital do indeed exist. What is more, it seems incautious to presume that what may be true for multiplayer online gamers – that is, gaming social capital creates offline social capital – applies to the general population of non-gamers.

We see a rough consensus in the relevant literature that the relationship between online social media, be they social networking sites or multiplayer gaming, and collective social capital is in general positive. As was the case with individual social capital, cultural and political contingencies may moderate the strength and pattern of the association between online social media and collective social capital.

Conclusion

What is online social capital? This should be the critical first question that researchers in this field have to ask when they conduct studies about the role of various social media. As we discussed in chapter 1, social capital as a concept has various definitions, none of which has succeeded in getting universal approval from the scientific community. This disorganized state of affairs is repeated in the studies of online social capital. Many studies have adopted a dichotomous categorization between bonding and bridging online social capitals without defining what online social capital itself is and clarifying how online social capital differs from offline social capital. Some studies have assumed the network-based perspective of social capital, although they rarely measure online social capital using a network generator – an exceptional case is Matzat and Sadowski (2015), who employed a resource generator especially for online contacts. In some sense, the majority of studies in the field have uncritically adopted a few widely known offline social capital theories and measurements.

In the execution of empirical studies, many researchers have used convenient small-sized samples, which make it hard to generalize their findings. Furthermore, they have mostly recruited college students, adolescents, or young adults as respondents. Although it is true that the young are more active users of social media, representative samples need to be developed that cover a wider age range because middle-aged and older adults also use mobile communication devices and social media.

Regarding the relationship between online social media and individual social capital, the empirical studies reviewed indicate in general that the internet, social media, online gaming, and mobile devices help maintain or extend personal networks. Realistically, those we converse with in online social media are mostly the persons with whom we have had physical contact in schools, neighborhoods, churches, temples, and synagogues, workplaces, and voluntary associations. It is right that online media facilitate social interactions in electronically engineered cyberspaces and may to some extent create new social ties that we are unable to contact without technological assistance. Nevertheless, it is farfetched to argue that online social media will eventually replace face-to-face social contact.

When considering an extreme case, it would be helpful to have a balanced view of social media and individual social capital. For instance, Facebook, a social media company, allows its users a maximum of 5,000 friends. Some hyper-social people complain about this restriction. Yet we might ask if it is even possible for a human being to maintain 5,000 friends concurrently – some may say there is no problem because Facebook friends are different from real friends. Dunbar (2016) dealt directly with this topic, comparing two nationally representative samples from the United Kingdom: the first sample was composed only of social media users and the second sample mixed social media users and nonusers. First, the average number of friends was 155 and 182 in the two samples respectively – note that the first sample of social media users reported a smaller mean number. Neither the network size nor the distributional shapes of the two samples differed significantly. Second, those who belonged to the first sample regarded only 28 per cent of their Facebook friends to be genuine or close friends. Third, when asked how many in their support clique comprising friends they could rely on for emotional support when in need and for the number of close friends they had, the first sample of social media users provided the means of 4 and 14, respectively. All these numbers are very small compared to the 5,000 Facebook friend maximum. What these results tell us, Dunbar (2016: 7) argues, is that, although online social media help people to be technically free from the time constraint of managing social ties, they still cannot overcome the cognitive constraint about the number of social ties. He explains further, "We can only interact coherently with a very small number of other people (about three, in fact) at any one time. It seems that even in an online environment, the focus of our attention is still limited in this way" (Dunbar 2016: 7).

With regard to the question of online social media and collective social capital, social media may be an enabler of mobilizing social resources, people, and the assets they possess for public causes. Thus social media's potential for promoting collective social capital should be recognized. What is generally missing in the relevant literature is the search for specific mechanisms by which voluntary associations recruit and maintain volunteers in online social media, rather than, or accompanied by, a traditional person-to-person approach to volunteer candidates. But it is hard to expect online social media to become the main producers of collective social capital because they are essentially profit-makers. Indeed, it may not be social media use that increases or decreases the level of trust toward most people in a society. What may matter more is what people experience and exchange with others on social media platforms. If they are exposed to more of the dark side of social relations through real-time online media, there is no reason to believe that the use of social media will promote trust.

7
Social Capital: Delimitation and Empowerment

Social capital relates to diverse areas such as civil society, economic development, status attainment, health, aging, mortality, and online social media, as we have observed in previous chapters. And there is more. This shows how popular social capital is. However, does it also indicate how good social capital is as a concept? Probably not. The virtue of a concept involves both reliability and validity. It is reliable when, for instance, repeated trials of the social capital measurement produce the same or very similar results. It is valid if the indicators of social capital represent the conceptual meaning of it coherently. As we have seen in previous chapters, many studies have used a wide variety of convenient indicators – roughly put, anything social, anything related to trust, or anything connecting ties and contacts was adamantly termed social capital – without justifying how such indicators represent social capital. Thus it may be meaningless to ask if they are reliable and valid measures because in the first place they were not created to measure social capital. This is why Li (2015: 1) criticizes the concept of social capital as there is "a risk that it is becoming over-general." This malpractice of using any measure of sociality as an indicator of social capital has ironically helped its widespread application in many fields. But not everything social is social capital. It is like calling any behavioral or psychological feature about politics political capital. Simply put, voting is voting, not political capital (unfortunately, voting is sometimes called social capital). Likewise, the frequency per week of saying hello to neighbors does not of itself represent social capital; rather, it shows a degree of prosocial behavior toward neighbors.

This concluding chapter deals with some critical issues related to the need to delimit the social capital concept. First, I discuss a representative problem that involves the relationship between social capital and trust, relying partly on Emile Durkheim's theory. Second, I briefly survey how the literature has exerted efforts to reconceptualize social capital. Lastly, I suggest a consolidated social capital model in which its preconditions, structural basis, and production form an organic relationship. The model delimits the social capital concept to empower it.

Delimitation: social capital and trust

The question of the reliability and validity of social capital concept brings us back to a fundamental subject discussed earlier in the book. What is social capital? Social capital is shared instrumental and expressive resources among people. Each person may possess his/her own resources. For these to be shared, mutual relations need to be formed in the first place. No relation, then no "social" capital. This is how the network-based or relation-based perspective of social capital came into being. The perspective argues forcefully that social capital must be embedded in interpersonal networks.

However, the story does not end there. For resources to be shared, there also needs to be either tacit or explicit agreement among people. Knowing one another does not automatically translate into sharing resources between them. A and B know each other; but they may be bitter enemies between whom only enmity is shared. The degree of shared resources should thus be agreed bilaterally, multilaterally, or collectively. This agreement may be, for Fukuyama, the instantiated informal norm and, for Putnam, norms of reciprocity (see Table 1.1). The relative ease of such sharing among weakly related people in America produced Mark Granovetter's (1973) proposition of the strength of weak ties. Conversely, the traditional norm that locks shared resources within particular groups in China made Yanjie Bian's (1997) counterargument of *guanxi*. Further, Karl Marx theorized that the total volume of material resources may be loosely cumulated only within capitalists, while Pierre Bourdieu maintained that so-called fungible assets do not spill over beyond the durable network of the ruling class (Table 1.1). Therefore, the agreement required for the existence and operation of shared resources can be both structural (e.g., class division) and cultural-historical (e.g., clan relations, highbrow class culture [cultural capital], American individualism).

Lastly, how far does agreement on sharing resources reach? Again, for Marx and Bourdieu it is confined to the upper class and hence resources do not cross over the class boundary. And in some collectivistic cultures resources are not usually exchanged between particular groups. This is why birth-ascribed status is crucial in those structural and cultural closures. However, such exclusive closures do not apply everywhere in the modern world and vary in degree across societies. Then how can we tell the extent of such an agreement? An implicit way to measure it may be to ask about trust. But trust is a fuzzy concept so I will not discuss it in depth. In short, when one trusts someone, it means one believes that person will at least not cause one harm. This is the baseline which does not yet involve any social exchange. Having such a belief may facilitate social exchange when the opportunity arises. For example, one believes that if one does someone a favor, the recipient will return it in the future. This belief, or trust, is related to the norms of reciprocity but is different from them. Norms exist, but one cannot be sure that the other party will follow the same norms. This can be likened to the fact that people in a country all know that they are bound by the law of the nation; but they also know that there are criminals among them. Thus trust helps initiate social exchange while risking a loss that may occur if the other party breaks the norms. Whether one can ask someone to look after one's money, house, shop, company, loved ones, or life on behalf of oneself is dependent on varying degrees of trust, which increase incrementally from baseline trust. In addition, some social exchanges, such as volunteer labor and philanthropy, do not require direct reciprocal action from their recipients. Rather, those behaviors widen the scope of sharing resources by expecting the recipients or the observers of the events to extend the favor to third parties in need. These are called generalized norms of reciprocity. And to initiate behaviors of generalized reciprocity with unknown people, trust toward strangers, or out-group trust, is a necessary condition.

Therefore, social capital, the shared resources in a social network, may be affected by the tacit or explicit agreements people make. Norms of reciprocity and trust comprise tacit agreement because they are derived from belief systems about social relations and exchange. Legal sanctions against misconducts are explicit agreements for they are forced by the state, based on the legal code incorporating penal and civil laws. Among these, legal sanctions – explicit agreement – are beyond the control of individuals because they are a given condition that applies in principle to every citizen in a country. Similarly, norms of reciprocity – tacit agreement – are part of customs, a product of culture and history, so that they are not easily modified by individuals. Thus both norms of reciprocity and legal sanctions may be regarded as constants in a social capital equation. Simply put, we have to take them as they are. The only variable among the three is trust, a part of tacit agreement, because each person may hold different degrees of trust toward others as he or she decides, although the overall level of trust in a group may affect each personal decision.

So it boils down to the relationship between trust and social capital. Trust, an indicator of tacit agreement about sharing resources, may facilitate social interaction and exchange with others, which can affect the amount of social capital. There are two crucial points in regard to this relationship. First, trust and social capital are separate conceptual entities, according to this network-based approach. Trust is exogenous to social capital. Trust is an attitude toward people. Social capital indicates the volume of instrumental and expressive resources within a network. In extreme cases, social capital can exist regardless of the degree or even the presence or absence of trust as long as there are operational ties. For example, as we observed in chapter 6, people rely on purchasing e-commerce products on the internet although they do not know nor trust sellers in person. People get paid rides from total strangers using Uber, Lyft, or Grab services, which might expose them to safety hazards (Etzioni 2017). Legal sanctions, the aforementioned explicit agreement, may intervene in case of malfeasance and compensate for the lack of trust. In other words, the possible intervention of legal sanctions prevents malfeasance in advance. Second, trust is one of the preconditions of social relations that form the structural basis of social capital. Belonging to a family, school, neighborhood, company, political party, class, or nation forms the structural foundation of social relations. Then trust provides a cultural-psychological impetus that facilitates certain types of relations within and between those social groupings. Not all the workers at a company nor all the students at a school become work colleagues or friends, respectively. Selective presence of relationships and relative degrees of intimacy among them are inevitable. Trust may work as a criterion for the selection of ties and adjustments to the levels of intimacy.

Trust, an indicator of tacit agreement about social relations and the possible sharing of resources, is a part of collective consciousness in Emile Durkheim's theoretical perspective (Durkheim 1933 [1893]). Although it allows individual variation, the object, the scope, and the overall level of trust are collectively arranged and thus may differ by social group. Collective consciousness was simpler to form and maintain prior to industrialization when mechanical solidarity prevailed among familial or pseudo-familial communities. Unified religions provided a fundamental belief system for the formation of collective consciousness among people sharing ethnicity, history, and culture within a geographical boundary. However, since the advent of industrialization, the influence of traditional social organization has weakened. Furthermore, the accompanying secularization deprived religions of their bonding function for the whole society. Instead, the division of labor and cooperation among a number of occupations reformulated an industrial social organization, producing organic solidarity among mutually unacquainted occupation holders who resided in different cities or even countries.

Collective consciousness may from time to time be jeopardized by deviant behaviors. Likewise, trust, a tacit agreement among people, is occasionally betrayed. Retaliation against betrayers takes an impersonal institutionalized form of codification in the civilized world. Both penal punishment and restitutive sanction may apply to cases of misdemeanor. The degree of legal punishment is proportional to the damages made against collective consciousness and "the institution of this power serves to maintain the collective conscience itself" (Durkheim 1933 [1893]: 104, a better translation of the French word *conscience* should be "consciousness" in this context). Hence the presence of explicit agreement in institutionalized forms of legal sanctions is mainly to protect the tacit agreement among social actors. And we know that it is costly to rely on legal procedures in any society. At any rate, either tacit agreement or explicit agreement should operate effectively in a population through voluntary consent among people or legal enforcement by the state. Otherwise, social relations are so restricted that social capital based on extensive and diverse social ties is depleted.

Treating trust as social capital stems from this communalist social theory. Trust, a tacit agreement between numerous agents and a form of collective consciousness among them, is one of the necessary conditions for the formation of collectivity. If one understands social capital in a figurative and symbolic way, detached from the concrete resources commonly held by a network of people, one may call trust social capital. Likewise, norms of reciprocity as a principal rule of social exchange may also be regarded as social capital in the broad sense of the term. Of course, a network-based theory of social capital refutes this idea because trust and norms are not resources in themselves. And whether to include these preconditions of social relations in the concept of social capital has been a key source of disagreement in the literature. Let us check what relevant studies have found or argued about the relationship between social capital and trust.

What the literature say about social capital and trust

Trust and norms of reciprocity may differ group by group (or even person by person). That is, the same set of trust and norms of reciprocity cannot be expected to apply universally across groups because each has its own principles and conditions of social organization. In addition, even within a group, trust and norms of reciprocity may fail to be accepted by most members. Thus Foley, Edwards, and Diani (2001) argue that trust and norms of reciprocity by themselves cannot be understood as social capital. But they take a mediatory position, asserting that when trust and norms are accepted by the majority of a group and thus have use value in that context, it is social capital. For instance, a neighborhood may have a norm of looking after unattended children. But it is not social capital unless the norm is accepted and followed by the majority of residents. The norm may turn to social capital if the residents can hold a natural expectation about protecting unattended children in the neighborhood. In this case, they argue, the norm acquires use value as a social capital. Likewise, trust may also have contextualized conditions by social groups and geographic units. Hence, it is not sound practice to use the grand mean of trust of the whole society as a measure of social capital because it cancels out the impacts of local social contexts. This argument suggests an alternative that trust and norms, the tacit agreement as preconditions of social relations, may be called social capital if they are highly likely to form and activate certain social resources (in this case, protection of children in the neighborhood).

Fischer (2005) was more critical of the concept of social capital itself and the relationship between social capital and trust in his review of Robert Putnam's *Bowling Alone*. First, he argues that the declining trend of social capital shown in the book seems an increasing trend of individualism in the United States. Second, criticizing the multifaceted concept and measurement of Putnam's social capital, he tested for coherence among seven indicators of social capital using an accumulated GSS (General Social Survey) data set between 1972 and 2000. Most of all, he suggests, "If these behaviors all reflected some underlying property of individuals – personal tendencies toward social connectedness and commitment – then we would expect people who generally do one behavior to also generally do another" (Fischer 2005: 158). However, the highest correlation coefficient among them was 0.27

between attendance at church services and the number of organization types a respondent belonged to, which is a modest association given that the coefficient can go up to 1.00. A strikingly problematic part is the correlations between trust and other indicators: voting (0.10), attendance (0.03), organizations (0.09), neighbors (0.04), friends (0.05), and giving (0.08). They are generally low and, in particular, the correlations of generalized trust with meeting friends and neighbors, indicators of social connection, were close to zero. These results warn that trust, among other things, should not be squeezed under the single rubric of social capital.

In the specific domain of health research, Carpiano and Fitterer (2014: 226) asked a simple but crucial question, "Is trust really social capital?" To test the relationship, they devised an empirical study using the 2008 Canadian General Social Survey in which both generalized trust and particular trust toward neighbors were employed along with measures of actual individual and organizational network, number of known ties (network diversity) from a position generator of 18 occupations and membership and participation in eight types of voluntary groups. The outcome measures were self-reported general health and mental health. The proposition they had was that if trust and network-based social capital are highly related, then the measures of trust should lose their effect when network measures are introduced to explain health outcomes. First, they found that both trust measures were found to be only modestly related to the network-based social capital measures. Second, when both trust measures and network-based social capital variables were considered concurrently in predicting health outcomes, trust remained significantly associated with general and mental health. In conclusion, they maintain, "Though one might argue that generalized and particularized trust are capturing the potential or willingness of a person to establish social ties and generate social capital with similar or dissimilar others ... this psychological state or disposition to engage with others is conceptually different from actually possessing social capital" (Carpiano and Fitterer 2014: 233). This is part of the reason that I define trust as a precondition of tacit agreement that may affect the formation of social relations.

However, Lindström (2014) put up a counterargument claiming that there are multiple definitions of social capital such as those from a network-based perspective that exclude trust (e.g., Bourdieu) and those from a social cohesion perspective that include trust (e.g., Putnam). Hence he did not agree with Carpiano and Fitterer's (2014) argument that social capital should be exclusively based on social networks. Next, he was against Carpiano and Fitter's proposition (2014) that trust and measures of networks should be highly correlated as coherent indicators of social capital. Instead, he argues that trust and networks can be independent from each other, referring to a Swedish study that showed different combinations between the two variables: that is, 42 percent of the randomly sampled adults reported a combination of high trust and high social participation, 27 percent reported low trust and high social participation, 15 percent had high trust and low social participation, and 16 percent had low trust and low participation. Lindström then argues, "it is not theoretically or conceptually obvious why membership in social networks and trust should be statistically highly associated with each other to such an extent that they would be expected to measure exactly the same phenomenon as perfect 'proxies' for each other" (Lindström 2014: 236). Next, he does not agree with the argument that trust is only a psychological trait. Citing the 1990–3 World Values Survey, he shows that only 7 percent in Brazil were generalized trusters, while in Sweden it was 66 percent. Then he argued that such a huge international difference may be largely due to structural and institutional, rather than psychological, causes. Based on this reasoning, he concludes that both the social cohesion and network perspectives of social capital should be considered by public health researchers. Likewise, Sawada (2014: 238) argues that trust complements social capital and thus "can therefore be regarded as an important component of social capital."

In reply to Lindström's criticism, Carpiano (2014) underlines that although studies of health acknowledge that there are multiple definitions of social capital, they disregard the various definitions of trust other than the perceived trust measures that they most frequently use. In particular, he elaborates, although Coleman (1990) and Putnam and colleagues (1993) included trust in their definitions of social capital, the trust they refer to is "the trust that an actor has with others in a group – i.e., *interpersonal* trust" (Carpiano 2014: 239, emphasis in the original). However, health studies usually employ generalized and particularized trust, attitude-based measures that reflect one's perception of one's social world, not interpersonal trust in real relations per se. In view of these multiple definitions of social capital and trust, Carpiano underscores that it is necessary to conduct empirical investigations to seek possible combinations of them. He is also critical of Lindström's argument as being logically inconsistent in that he maintains, according to seminal social capital definitions (Coleman 1990; Putnam, Leonardi, and Nanetti 1993), that trust should conceptually be a part of social capital, and yet he argues that trust and social capital do not need to be correlated. This series of discussions vividly mirror the conflicted status of network-based and social cohesion perspectives of social capital. Interestingly, the editor who invited these commentaries in the same issue of the journal was Ichiro Kawachi. Although he introduced the social cohesion perspective of social capital in health research (see chapter 5), he seems to have realized the need to reconsider it in light of the network-based perspective.

Then would there be different associations between interpersonal trust and social capital than between perceived trust and social capital as Carpiano (2014) surmises? Son and Feng (2019) tested the relationship using nationally representative data sets from the United States and China. They proposed three theoretical perspectives regarding the relationship between social capital and trust: the compositional element perspective (Putnam) that subsumes trust along with network and norms of reciprocity; the functional equivalence perspective (Fukuyama) that treats trust and social capital alike; and the mutual independence perspective (Lin) that assumes no relationship between them. In testing each perspective, they used interpersonal trust (network trust) and perceived trust (generalized trust) for measuring trust, and position generators and organizational memberships for measuring individual and organizational social capital. First, individual social capital was negatively related to interpersonal trust in both countries. They explained that to expand individual social capital, people should reach out beyond the boundary of trusted persons. In other words, those who hunker down with only trustworthy others tend to form smaller social networks and social capital. Second, there was no relation between individual social capital and generalized trust. This may indicate that the perception of most people does not have anything to do with individual social capital because it is a psychological trait, not a specific evaluation of actual persons. Third, organizational social capital, the number of memberships in voluntary associations, was significantly related to generalized trust in the United States but not in China. This shows that the assumption of tight coupling between trust and civic engagement may be a product of American civic culture which is not applicable to other countries. In conclusion, these results confirm that trust is not a component of social capital nor equal to it.

Apart from how to situate the relationship between social capital and trust, innate problems with generalized trust and its measurement were also criticized by some empirical studies. Reeskens and Hooghe (2008) indicate that there is ambiguity in the question of generalized trust with regard to who respondents have in mind when they are asked if they trust "most people." Hence the question may not be fit for cross-cultural comparative studies. Sturgis and Smith (2010) devised a concrete way to examine the validity of the generalized trust question. They employed two conditions in a British survey: half of the respondents were asked a generalized trust question, while the other half were asked an alternative question about trust toward people in the local area. Immediately after the trust items were put to them, both sets of respondents were asked who came to mind when they were thinking about "most people" or "people in the local area." First, 48 percent of the respondents who encountered the generalized trust question indicated that most people can be trusted, while 80 percent of the respondents who responded to the alternative question answered that they trusted people in the local area. This shows that reduction in the geographical scope produced a higher level of trust. Second, the respondents who called to mind people known to them when they answered the generalized trust question were four and a half times more likely to indicate that most people can be trusted, relative to others who thought of people in general. These results show that the generalized trust question can indeed be interpreted in two different ways. The question may not measure what it intends to.

Furthermore, Torpe and Lolle (2011) found that the standard question on generalized trust is perceived differently depending on which part of the world the respondents belong to. Although the generalized trust question is supposed to measure trust in strangers, people in certain regions are more likely to think of persons known to them when they respond to the generalized trust question. They used the 2006–8 WVS (World Values Survey) that asked various questions on trust including the standard generalized trust and the question of trust in strangers. Specifically, in Asian countries 74 percent of those who indicated "most people can be trusted" reported not trusting those they meet for the first time. This was 65 percent in the former Eastern bloc, 60 percent in Africa, and 56 percent in Latin America. In Western Europe it was lowest at 33 percent. That is, three-fourths of Asian respondents who answered positively to the generalized trust question referred to particular persons they knew. Therefore, comparative studies between different regions that used the standard generalized trust question may have reported biased results. Using the same WVS data, Delhey, Newton, and Welzel (2011) also report that the actual radii of most people vary substantially across regions and countries and are significantly narrower in countries with a Confucian culture, such as South Korea and China. And they found that the wider the trust radius, the greater the civicness.

This section has put various arguments with regard to the relationship between social capital and trust, a highly debated topic in the literature. Now we turn to alternative conceptualizations of social capital and the disputes concerning them.

Alternative conceptualizations of social capital

How to define and conceptualize social capital has become a critical issue in whichever discipline social capital entered. And it has caused similar struggles surrounding its catchall nature. For instance, Adler and Kwon (2002) have provided a conceptual framework of social capital to be used in management studies. And the framework reflects the intrinsic problem of social capital – overloading on a single concept.

They suggest that the sources of social capital can be traced to the social structure to which actors belong (Adler and Kwon 2002: 18). They broke social structure down into three dimensions: the market relations of exchanging goods and services for money; the hierarchical relations within organizations; and the social relations of exchanging favors. They presumed, among these, that social relations are the basis of the social structure producing the other two relational dimensions. Social relations may produce social capital when they encounter proper opportunity structures, along with the right motivation (transactional norms) and ability of contacts. Next, social capital produces either benefits in the forms of information, influence, power, control, and solidarity, or risks such as free-riding problems. Lastly, the value of social capital may be affected by contextual factors such as task contingency (e.g., selective use of weak or strong ties), symbolic contingency (e.g., norms and values), and complementary capabilities (e.g., ability to generate innovation based on ideas gathered by social capital). Although this article provided a general research framework of social capital tailored to management studies, it fell into the trap of having a catchall conceptualization. In particular, the framework does not clarify what social capital includes and excludes. A few relevant questions are as follows. Are norms, ability of contacts, or opportunities a part of social capital or separate from it? Are free-riding problems a part of social capital or its consequence? Is it not that solidarity, a structural characteristic, produces social capital, rather than the other way around?

Glanville and Bienenstock (2009) suggest another framework explicating how various forms of social capital interlink. They argue that despite the conceptual confusion about social capital, its diverse forms may take their places along four continua: "(a) dense to dispersed social networks, (b) level of trust and/or reciprocity, (c) level of resources, and (d) micro to macro" (Glanville and Bienenstock 2009: 1508). They propose that locating different types of social capital along these continua may enable a systematic comparison between them. Also, the consequences of a given form of social capital depend on its location along these continua. This study was another attempt to synthesize discrete theoretical entities under the umbrella conceptualization of social capital, although it provides a useful framework for considering different forms of social capital altogether.

Another concern was how to theorize a relationship between individual and collective social capitals. Rostila (2011) suggests that there are two major theoretical approaches: social capital as an individual good and social capital as an ecological characteristic. He then points out, "collective definitions of social capital do not pay much attention to the fact that individuals may possess and benefit from their social capital while individual notions often disregard the fact that coordinated actions by individuals in a social structure may ... produce (social) resources over and above individual's social capital" (Rostila 2011: 315). Therefore, he has devised a framework to link these two types of social capital. Specifically, he argues that social networks produce cognitive dimension of trust that in turn creates both collective and individual social resources. And these resources yield both instrumental and expressive returns. In support of this consolidated view, he argues that social capital is composed of "the social resources that evolve in accessible social networks and social structures characterized by mutual trust" (Rostila 2011: 321). I find it a problem that social networks produce social capital only through trust, when some studies report that networks are weakly or not associated with trust in the first place. Neither has it been clarified if the relationship between trust and individual and collective social capital is robust.

Bjørnskov and Sønderskov (2013) doubt if social capital is a good concept. Two salient criteria of a good concept are coherence and differentiation. Coherence means "the degree of internal coherence between the different attributes as well as between the actual, observable components of the concept," while differentiation refers to "the degree of boundedness from other, neighboring concepts" (Bjørnskov and Sønderskov 2013: 1230–1). Therefore, if the components of social capital, trust, norms, and networks as identified by

Putnam form an internally coherent concept, it should then be distinct from other existing concepts. They conducted a series of principal components analyses (PCA) at the individual and aggregate level, using data from 48 American states and 48 countries. Specifically, they ran a PCA on 20 items in the US data that are relevant to indicate Putnam's social capital concept. If the items measure social capital coherently, PCA should produce an overarching single component. Instead, PCA produced six different components at the individual level, such as involvement in local community, informal socialization, cultural activities, or sports activities. Likewise, PCA produced five separate dimensions from the social capital indicators at the aggregate level. International data from the WVS produced similar results. Hence, they conclude that the regularly operationalized components of Putnam's social capital concept fail to form a coherent scale. The different components are distinct entities with little in common. Additionally, they stress that the social capital concept "may have done damage to neighboring concepts by drawing them under one 'hat' and thereby distracting attention from these concepts" (Bjørnskov and Sønderskov 2013: 1239).

An example of this damage is the concept of social cohesion. There exists a social cohesion perspective of social capital, particularly in health studies, which stemmed from the theoretical approach of James Coleman and Robert Putnam that emphasized the benefits of cohesive communal bonding with a higher level of trust. Then what is the relationship between social cohesion and social capital? Carrasco and Bilal (2016) argue that social cohesion became unnecessarily conflated with social capital. The appearance of the social cohesion concept in health research originated with Emile Durkheim's *Suicide* which argued that higher suicide rates in Protestant countries vis-à-vis Catholic countries were significantly due to weaker social cohesion in the former. In subsequent studies, social cohesion was typically indicated by, among other things, trust, reciprocity, solidarity, equity, and social inclusion. Recall that some of these are indicators of social capital as well. Although social cohesion and its indicators did not have any place in the theory of Bourdieu (1986), who defined social capital as resources available within a class through networks of mutual acquaintance, Coleman and Putnam adopted social cohesion in conceptualizing social capital when they defined social capital as trust, information, or norms of reciprocity. And this compositional view of social capital overlaps with social cohesion, even to the extent that social capital includes social cohesion within its compass. This case exemplifies how a catchall definition of social capital encroaches on neighboring concepts.

Social capital: preconditions, structural basis, and production

Thus far, in this chapter and others, we have seen the merits and demerits of a comprehensive concept of social capital. The comprehensive conceptualization facilitated the adoption of social capital in various areas. For instance, social capital practically took a role of representing the impact of general sociality on economic development, population health, or status attainment. However, the ambiguity residing in the concept became a barrier to a clear understanding of what social capital is and what it can or cannot do.

Therefore, I suggested in chapter 1 that the division between individual and collective social capital is necessary to reduce the ambiguity, and accordingly I categorized the contributions of key social capital scholars following the typology. Then, earlier in this chapter, I proposed a delimited model of social capital. Specifically, it follows a procedural development of three steps: preconditions, structural basis, and production (Figure 7.1).

The model enforces two critical delimitations. First, it does not include the consequences of social capital (Woolcock 1998). This is crucial because many previous studies failed to differentiate between social capital and its consequences – for instance, civic engagement should be a product of social capital without being conflated with it. But numerous studies have treated civic engagement as equivalent to social capital. In addition, it is necessary to eliminate the consequences of social capital from the model because they have been mostly

Figure 7.1. A Delimited Model of Social Capital: Preconditions, Structural Basis, and Production

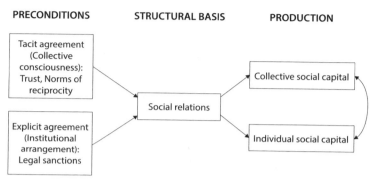

depicted as positive externalities, although it is plausible that social capital also produces negative consequences. Extreme examples may be organized crime and war: social capital is no doubt at its highest level in the mafia and in Islamic State (IS). And we know how these harm others using strong within-group bonding. But rarely does the literature of social capital take those negative externalities seriously, although it has been hinted here and there that there can be a dark side to it. It is almost as if social capital produces only good things. In a critical sense, chapters 3–6 reflect this lopsided nature of the literature.

Second, the model detaches the preconditions of social relations from social capital. As explained above, the preconditions of social relations are cultural-historical-institutional-psychological contextual factors that may help form or prevent certain types of social ties. Although these preconditions may affect the structural basis of social relations, they exist separately from individuals, their networks, and the embedded resources in the networks. The preconditions include both tacit and explicit agreements. Tacit agreement denotes the informal norms and rules of social relations, which should not be considered lightly because they have stood the test of time, becoming part of culture and history. This agreement may provide a guideline regarding whom to associate with and to what degree people may conduct social exchanges between themselves, believing that they belong to the same societal entity. This is what Durkheim (1933 [1893]) described as collective consciousness, which governs individuals in a society generating a sense of community, "we-ness," and morality. Through his later work on the totemic religions in Australia, he argues more forcefully, "There can be no society that does not experience the need at regular intervals to maintain and strengthen the collective feelings and ideas that provide its coherence and its distinct individuality" (Durkheim 1995 [1912]: 429). This argument does not only fall under the purview of religion but can apply to any fundamental belief system that holds a society together. And trust and norms of reciprocity may be indicative of the collective consciousness shared by a community. On the other hand, explicit agreement is an institutional arrangement that buttresses the role of tacit agreement by providing legal means to suppress and punish deviance and malfeasance. It should therefore be subsidiary to tacit agreement in principle. Nevertheless, it may play a major role in creating, maintaining, and voiding social relations and exchanges when the tacit agreement is underdeveloped or frail. For instance, in societies where informal trust is too weak and norms of reciprocity are frequently broken, legal institutions have to intervene as the principal guardians of social relations.

With these delimitations in place, the structural basis of social relations is formed. And the types and the degree of robustness of the basis may differ from one society to another, depending on what kind of tacit and explicit agreements they have developed. It is called a "structural" basis because connections and disconnections in the relations between individuals build a particular form of network structure tailored to each society. Then various resources belonging to each individual may be held and shared by the network structure. The structural basis does not include the preconditions of tacit and explicit agreements. Instead, the basis is a form constructed by those preconditions. Once formed, social interactions and exchanges – including the contents and volume of social exchanges – within the structural basis are executed in line with the prescribed behavioral rules set by the preconditions.

The structural basis of social relations can be constituted at two levels: individual and collective. Social relations at the individual level are the ones that belong to interpersonal networks. In principle, each person has the freedom to knit his or her own relational network incorporating those persons they choose to associate with. In other words, each person decides whom to include or exclude from the interpersonal network, the degree of interactional strength with others, the frequency of interactions with them, and what to exchange with them. Such interpersonal networks produce individual social capital as their embedded resources. Likewise, social relations at the collective level are those situated within organizational networks. Apart from family, the primary unit of sociality, societies tend to establish various secondary groups to satisfy certain collective needs and goals.

Some, not all, persons in a society opt into the secondary groups because belonging to those groups is not mandatory in the first place in most societies nor attractive, due to the cost of membership in terms of the investments of time, money, and other resources. There is no one who does not have an interpersonal network insofar as one lives in a society. But it is possible that the majority of people in a society do not belong to a collective network of secondary groups. These secondary groups are mainly for pursuing collective goals, in the process sometimes sacrificing personal interests. And this is why Robert Putnam was so concerned about the reduction in the rates of voluntary associational membership in the United States. In short, belonging to collective networks of secondary groups generates collective social capital, comprising both the organizational assets and personal resources of those who connect themselves to collective networks.

Ultimately, individual and collective social capitals, the products of social relations, may reinforce each other. Those who are replete with individual social capital are more likely to get involved in the communal matters of secondary groups by being asked by some of their network alters than others with deficient individual social capital (Musick and Wilson 2008). Thus the amount of individual social capital may be an indirect indicator of collective social capital, although, of course, not always so. Once attached to collective networks, people may have a greater chance of expanding their inter-personal networks by incorporating the ties they encounter in collective settings. Therefore, an enlargement of social capital circulating back and forth between individual and collective levels may take place. Nevertheless, in a negative scenario, a downward spiral may ensue due to a disconnection between insufficient individual and collective social capitals.

There is one outstanding issue to be clarified. In terms of the measurement of individual and collective social capitals, chapter 2 explained that the latter has usually been indicated by trust and membership in voluntary associations. In accordance with the delimited social capital model proposed in this chapter, trust is ineligible as an indicator of collective social capital because it is part of the preconditions two steps before the production of social capital. Yet chapter 2's purpose was to detail the status quo of the literature in terms of the measurement of social capital. It is also true that a majority of social capital studies have regarded trust as a measure of social capital. Is that the wrong thing to do? If one subscribes to this delimited model of social capital, the answer should be that it is a wrong practice. However, if one prefers a compositional view of social capital that subsumes trust, it is not wrong. Nevertheless, we may need to inquire seriously which perspective is more likely to help sustain the value of social capital as a social scientific concept in future studies.

Concluding remark

As a key concept in the social sciences, social capital is a product of these three questions. First, who are we? Second, why is it that we are who we are? Third, what is good or bad in who we are? In short, social capital is produced not by "I-ness," but by "we-ness." Thus the concept of social capital is deeply rooted in the Durkheimian sociological tradition that asks how it is possible for society to exist.

Neither individual social capital, composed of shared resources belonging to an interpersonal network, nor collective social capital, made up of common group assets and personal resources belonging to organizational networks, is possible without "we-ness" to a lesser or greater extent.

Nevertheless, it has been a widespread practice to ascertain that social capital should be beneficial to "my" job, earnings, education, physical health and mental well-being, or even communal living that "I" want to enjoy. Somehow, social capital has provided a self-centered view of social relations to the extent that it may be called personal monopolization of shared social resources. As economic capital, human capital, and cultural capital are used to maximize the gains that "I" and "my particular group or class" will get, so is social capital exploited to get ahead of others realizing personal advantages. This is wrong. Social capital may produce such personal or particularistic gains. However, social capital exists for all of those who belong to a common network, not for a specific focal person or a subgroup. Therefore, it is not correct to state, "I own social capital" or "I possess more social capital than you." One should instead say, "I am a part of social capital," not to sound self-effacing but to accurately reflect reality.

Although "we-ness" – in other words, "who are we?", not "who am I?" – forms the basis of social capital, it is also true that people compose different social networks by various reasons and end up with varying degrees of social resources embedded in them. In the process of joining or avoiding certain networks, people help clarify the characteristics of "we-ness" they construct or offer the reasons why they had to create a specific interpersonal or collective network. The main argument of social capital is that the selective belonging to "we-ness" in interpersonal or organizational networks and the resulting production of resources embedded in them may make a significant difference, either positive or negative, in diverse areas of life for those who subscribe to the social structural basis.

References

Adjaye-Gbewonyo, Kaful, Kawachi, Ichiro, Subramanian, Sankaran V., and Avendano, Mauricio. 2018. "High Social Trust Associated with Increased Depressive Symptoms in a Longitudinal South African Sample." *Social Science & Medicine* 197: 127–35.

Adler, Paul S. and Kwon, Seok-Woo. 2002. "Social Capital: Prospects for a New Concept." *Academy of Management Review* 27: 17–40.

Aguilera, Michael B. 2008. "Personal Networks and the Incomes of Men and Women in the United States: Do Personal Networks Provide Higher Returns for Men or Women?" *Research on Social Stratification and Mobility* 26: 221–33.

Aguilera, Michael B. and Massey, Douglas S. 2003. "Social Capital and the Wages of Mexican Migrants New Hypotheses and Tests." *Social Forces* 82: 671–701.

Aharony, Noa. 2015. "What's App: A Social Capital Perspective." *Online Information Review* 39: 26–42.

Ahlerup, Pelle, Olsson, Ola, and Yanagizawa, David. 2009. "Social Capital vs Institutions in the Growth Process." *European Journal of Political Economy* 25: 1–14.

Ahn, June. 2012. "Teenagers' Experiences with Social Network Sites: Relationships to Bridging and Bonding Social Capital." *The Information Society* 28: 99–109.

Aida, Jun, Hanibuchi, Tomoya, Nakade, Miyo, Hirai, Hiroshi, Osaka, Ken, and Kondo, Katsunori. 2009. "The Different Effects of Vertical Social Capital and Horizontal Social Capital on Dental Status: A Multilevel Analysis." *Social Science & Medicine* 69: 512–18.

Aida, Jun, Kondo, Katsunori, Kawachi, Ichiro, Subramanian, Sankaran V., et al. 2013. "Does Social Capital Affect the Incidence of Functional Disability in Older Japanese? A Prospective Population-based Cohort Study." *Journal of Epidemiology and Community Health* 67: 42–7.

Anderson, Alistair R. and Jack, Sarah L. 2002. "The Articulation of Social Capital in Entrepreneurial Networks: A Glue or a Lubricant?" *Entrepreneurship & Regional Development* 14: 193–210.

Anderson, Cameron and Cowan, Jon. 2014. "Personality and Status Attainment: A Micropolitics Perspective," in J. Cheng, J. Tracy, and C. Anderson (eds), *The Psychology of Social Status*. New York: Springer, pp. 99–117.

Appel, Lora, Dadlani, Punit, Dwyer, Maria, et al. 2014. "Testing the Validity of Social Capital Measures in the Study of Information and Communication Technologies." *Information, Communication & Society* 17: 398–416.

Baron, Stephen, Field, John, and Schuller, Tom (eds). 2000. *Social Capital: Critical Perspectives*. Oxford: Oxford University Press.

Bartkus, Viva O. and Davis, James H. 2009. *Social Capital: Reaching Out, Reaching In*. Cheltenham: Edward Elgar.

Bearman, Peter and Parigi, Paolo. 2004. "Cloning Headless Frogs and Other Important Matters: Conversation Topics and Network Structure." *Social Forces* 83: 535–57.

Beggs, John J. and Hurlbert, Jeanne S. 1997. "The Social Context of Men's and Women's Job Search Ties: Membership in Voluntary Organizations, Social Resources, and Job Search Outcomes." *Sociological Perspectives* 40: 601–22.

Behtoui, Alireza. 2007. "The Distribution and Return of Social Capital: Evidence from Sweden." *European Societies* 9: 383–407.

Benton, Richard A. 2016. "Uniters or Dividers? Voluntary Organizations and Social Capital Acquisition." *Social Networks* 44: 209–18.

Berman, Sheri. 1997. "Civil Society and the Collapse of the Weimar Republic." *World Politics* 49: 401–29.

Bertrand, Marianne and Mullainathan, Sendhil. 2004. "Are Emily and Greg More Employable than Lakisha and Jamal? A Field Experiment on Labor Market Discrimination." *American Economic Review* 94: 991–1013.

Beugelsdijk, Sjoerd and van Schaik, Ton. 2005. "Social Capital and Growth in European Regions: An Empirical Test." *European Journal of Political Economy* 21: 301–24.

Bian, Yanjie. 1997. "Bringing Strong Ties Back in: Indirect Ties, Network Bridges, and Job Searches in China." *American Sociological Review* 62: 366–85.

Bian, Yanjie. 2012. "Network Social Capital and Civic Engagement in Environmentalism in China," in A. Daniere, and H. V. Luong (eds), *The Dynamics of Social Capital and Civic Engagement in Asia*. London: Routledge, pp. 37–53.

Bian, Yanjie. 2019. *Guanxi: How China Works*. Cambridge: Polity Press.

Bian, Yanjie and Ang, Soon. 1997. "Guanxi Networks and Job Mobility in China and Singapore." *Social Forces* 75: 981–1005.

Bian, Yanjie, Huang, Xianbi, and Zhang, Lei. 2015. "Information and Favoritism: the Network Effect on Wage Income in China" *Social Networks* 40: 129–38.

Bjørnskov, Christian. 2003. "The Happy Few: Cross-country Evidence on Social Capital and Life Satisfaction." *Kyklos* 56: 3–16.

Bjørnskov, Christian and Sønderskov, Kim M. 2013. "Is Social Capital a Good Concept?" *Social Indicators Research* 114: 1225–42.

Blau, Peter M. and Duncan, Otis D. 1967. *The American Occupational Structure*. New York: John Wiley & Sons.

Boase, Jeffrey and Ikeda, Ken'ichi. 2012. "Core Discussion Networks in Japan and America." *Human Communication Research* 38: 95–119.

Bourdieu, Pierre. 1980. "Le Capital Social: Notes Provisoires." *Actes de la Recherche en Sciences Sociales* 3: 2–3.

Bourdieu, Pierre. 1984. *Distinction: A Social Critique of the Judgement of Taste*. Cambridge, MA: Harvard University Press.

Bourdieu, Pierre. 1986. "The Forms of Capital," in J. G. Richardson (ed.), *Handbook of Theory and Research for the Sociology of Education*, Westport, CT: Greenwood Press, pp. 241–58.

Breen, Richard and Jonsson, Jan. O. 2005. "Inequality of Opportunity in Comparative Perspective: Recent Research on Educational Attainment and Social Mobility." *Annual Review of Sociology* 31: 223–43.

Burt, Ronald S. 1984. "Network Items and the General Social Survey." *Social Networks* 6: 293–339.

Burt, Ronald S. 1992. *Structural Holes: The Social Structure of Competition*. Cambridge, MA: Harvard University Press.

Burt, Ronald. 2000. "The Network Structure of Social Capital." *Research in Organizational Behavior* 22: 345–423.

Buttrick, Steven C. and Moran, John P. 2005. "Russia's Missing Link? Social Capital, Entrepreneurialism, and Economic Performance in Post-communist Russia." *Communist and Post-Communist Studies* 38: 357–68.

Campbell, Karen E. and Lee, Barrett A. 1991. "Name Generators in Surveys of Personal Networks." *Social Networks* 13: 203–21.

Campos-Matos, Ines, Subramanian, Sankaran V., and Kawachi, Ichiro. 2016. "The 'Dark Side' of Social Capital: Trust and Self-rated Health in European Countries." *European Journal of Public Health* 26: 90–5.

Cappellari, Lorenzo and Tatsiramos, Konstantinos. 2015. "With a Little Help from My Friends? Quality of Social Networks, Job Finding and Job Match Quality." *European Economic Review* 78: 55–75.

Carothers, Thomas and Barndt, William. 1999. "Civil Society." *Foreign Policy* 117: 18–29.

Carpiano, Richard M. 2006. "Toward a Neighborhood Resource-based Theory of Social Capital for Health: Can Bourdieu and Sociology Help?" *Social Science & Medicine* 62: 165–75.

Carpiano, Richard M. 2007. "Neighborhood Social Capital and Adult Health: An Empirical Test of a Bourdieu-based Model." *Health & Place* 13: 639–55.

Carpiano, Richard M. 2014. "When Should One (Dis)trust Trust Measures? Response to Lindström and Sawada." *Social Science & Medicine* 116: 239–40.

Carpiano, Richard M. and Fitterer, Lisa M. 2014. "Questions of Trust in Health Research on Social Capital: What Aspects of Personal Network Social Capital Do They Measure?" *Social Science & Medicine* 116: 225–34.

Carrasco, Maria A. and Bilal, Usama. 2016. "A Sign of the Times: To Have or to Be? Social Capital or Social Cohesion." *Social Science & Medicine* 159: 127–31.

Casey, Terrance and Christ, Kevin. 2005. "Social Capital and Economic Performance in the American States." *Social Science Quarterly* 86: 826–45.

Chan, Michael. 2015. "Mobile Phones and the Good Life: Examining the Relationships among Mobile Use, Social Capital and Subjective Well-Being." *New Media & Society* 17: 96–113.

Chen, Hsuan-Ting and Li, Xueqing. 2017. "The Contribution of Mobile Social Media to Social Capital and Psychological Well-being: Examining the Role of Communicative Use, Friending and Self-disclosure." *Computers in Human Behavior* 75: 958–65.

Chen, Jie and Lu, Chunlong. 2007. "Social Capital in Urban China: Attitudinal and Behavioral Effects on Grassroots Self-Government." *Social Science Quarterly* 88: 422–42.

Chen, Yunsong and Volker, Beate. 2016. "Social Capital and Homophily Both Matter for Labor Market Outcomes – Evidence from Replication and Extension." *Social Networks* 45: 18–31.

Choi, Sejung Marina, Kim, Yoojung, Sung, Yongjun, and Sohn, Dongyoung. 2010. "Bridging or Bonding? A Cross-cultural Study of Social Relationships in Social Networking Sites." *Information, Communication & Society* 14: 107–29.

Chua, Vincent. 2011. "The Contingent Value of Unmobilized Social Capital in Getting a Good Job." *Sociological Perspectives* 57: 124–43.

Cobb, Sidney. 1976. "Social Support as a Moderator of Life Stress." *Psychosomatic Medicine* 38: 300–14.

Coleman, James S. 1961. *The Adolescent Society: The Social Life of the Teenager and Its Impact on Education.* New York: Free Press.

Coleman, James S. 1988. "Social Capital in the Creation of Human Capital." *American Journal of Sociology* 94: S95–S120.

Coleman, James S. 1990. *Foundations of Social Theory.* Cambridge, MA: Belknap Press of Harvard University Press.

Croezen, Simone, Avendano, Mauricio, Burdorf, Alex, and van Lenthe, Frank J. 2015. "Social Participation and Depression in Old Age: A Fixed-Effects Analysis in 10 European Countries." *American Journal of Epidemiology* 182: 168–76.

Cross, Jennifer L. Moren and Lin, Nan. 2008. "Access to Social Capital and Status Attainment in the United States: Racial/Ethnic and Gender Differences," in N. Lin and B. H. Erickson (eds), *Social Capital: An International Research Program.* New York: Oxford University Press, pp. 364–79.

Dalton, Robert J. and Ong, Nhu-Ngoc N. T. 2004. "Civil Society and Social Capital in Vietnam," in Rainer Klump and Gerhard Mutz (eds), *Modernization and Social Change in Vietnam.* Munich: Munich Institute for Social Science.

Dasgupta, Partha and Serageldin, Ismail (eds) 2000. *Social Capital: A Multifaceted Perspective.* Washington, DC: The World Bank.

Day, Kathleen and Devlin, Rose Anne. 1997. "Can Volunteer Work Help Explain the Male–Female Earnings Gap?" *Applied Economics* 29: 707–21.

De Graaf, Dirk Nan and Flap, Hendrik Derk. 1988. "'With a Little Help from My Friends': Social Resources as an Explanation of Occupational Status and Income in West Germany, the Netherlands, and the United States." *Social Forces* 67: 452–72.

De Ulzurrun, Laura Morales Diez. 2002. "Associational Membership and Social Capital in Comparative Perspective: A Note on the Problems of Measurement." *Politics & Society* 30: 497–523.

Dekker, Paul and Van den Broek, Andries. 1998. "Civil Society in Comparative Perspective: Involvement in Voluntary Associations in North America and Western Europe." *Voluntas* 9: 11–38.

Delhey, Jan, Newton, Kenneth, and Welzel, Christian. 2011. "How

General is Trust in "Most People"? Solving the Radius of Trust Problem." *American Sociological Review* 76: 786–807.

Diez de Ulzurrun, Laura Morales. 2002. "Associational Membership and Social Capital in Comparative Perspective: A Note on the Problems of Measurement." *Politics & Society* 30: 497–523.

Doh, Soogwan. 2014. "Social Capital, Economic Development, and the Quality of Government: How Interaction between Social Capital and Economic Development Affects the Quality of Government." *Public Administration* 92: 104–24.

Dudwick, Nora, Kuehnast, Kathleen, Nyhan Jones, Veronica, and Woolcock, Michael. 2006. *Analyzing Social Capital in Context: A Guide to Using Qualitative Methods and Data*. Washington, DC: World Bank Institute.

Dunbar, Robin I. M. 2016. "Do Online Social Media Cut Through the Constraints that Limit the Size of Offline Social Networks?" *Royal Society Open Science* 3. DOI: 10.1098/rsos.150292.

Durkheim, Emile. 1933 [1893]. *The Division of Labor in Society*. New York: The Free Press.

Durkheim, Emile. 1995 [1912]. *The Elementary Forms of the Religious Life*, trans. K. E. Fields. New York: The Free Press.

Durlauf, Steven N. and Fafchamps, Marcel. 2004. *Social Capital*. Cambridge, MA: National Bureau of Economic Research

Działek, Jarosław. 2014. "Is Social Capital Useful for Explaining Economic Development in Polish Regions?" *Geografiska Annaler; Series B, Human Geography* 96: 177–93.

Ellison, Nicole B., Steinfield, Charles, and Lampe, Cliff. 2007. "The Benefits of Facebook 'Friends': Social Capital and College Students' Use of Online Social Network Sites." *Journal of Computer-Mediated Communication* 12: 1143–68.

Ellison, Nicole B., Vitak, Jessica, Gray, Rebecca, and Lampe, Cliff. 2014. "Cultivating Social Resources on Social Network Sites: Facebook Relationship Maintenance Behaviors and Their Role in Social Capital Processes." *Journal of Computer-Mediated Communication* 19: 855–70.

Erickson, Bonnie H. 2001. "Good Networks and Good Jobs: The Value of Social Capital to Employers and Employees" in N. Lin, K. Cook, and R. S. Burt (eds), *Social Capital: Theory and Research*. New York: Aldine de Gruyter, pp. 127–58.

Eriksson, Malin and Ng, Nawi. 2015. "Changes in Access to Structural Social Capital and Its Influence on Self-rated Health Over Time for Middle-aged Men and Women: A Longitudinal Study from Northern Sweden." *Social Science & Medicine* 130: 250–8.

Esser, Hartmut. 2008. "The Two Meanings of Social Capital," in D. Castiglione, J. W. Van Deth, and G. Wolleb (eds), *The Handbook of Social Capital*. Oxford: Oxford University Press, pp. 22–49.

Etzioni, Amitai. 2017. "Cyber Trust." *Journal of Business Ethics* 1–13. https://doi.org/10.1007/s10551-017-3627-y.

Evans, Peter B. 1995. *Embedded Autonomy: States and Industrial Transformation*. Princeton, NJ: Princeton University Press.

Evans, Peter B. 1996. "Government Action, Social Capital and Development: Reviewing the Evidence on Synergy." *World Development* 24: 1119–32.

Farr, James. 2004. "Social Capital: A Conceptual History." *Political Theory* 32: 6–33.

Faucher, Kane X. 2018. *Social Capital Online: Alienation and Accumulation*. London: University of Westminster Press.

Featherman, David L. and Hauser, Robert M. 1976. "Prestige or Socioeconomic Scales in the Study of Occupational Achievement?" *Sociological Methods & Research* 4: 403–22.

Featherman, David L., Lancaster Jones, F., and Hauser, Robert M. 1975. "Assumptions of Social Mobility Research in the US: The Case of Occupational Status." *Social Science Research* 4: 329–60.

Ferlander, Sara. 2007. "The Importance of Different Forms of Social Capital for Health." *Acta Sociologica* 50: 115–28.

Fernandez, Roberto M., Castilla, Emilio J., and Moore, Paul. 2000. "Social Capital at Work: Networks and Employment at a Phone Center." *American Journal of Sociology* 105: 1288–356.

Field, John. 2008. *Social Capital*. New York: Routledge.

Fischer, Claude S. 1982. *To Dwell Among Friends: Personal Networks in Town and City*. Chicago: University of Chicago Press.

Fischer, Claude S. 2005. "Bowling Alone: What's the Score?" *Social Networks* 27: 155–67.

Fischer, Claude S. 2009. "The 2004 GSS Findings of Shrunken Social Networks: An Artifact?" *American Sociological Review* 74: 657–69.

Foley, Michael W. and Edwards, Bob. 1998. "Beyond Tocqueville: Civil Society and Social Capital in Comparative Perspective: Editor's Introduction." *American Behavioral Scientist* 42: 5–20.

Foley, Michael W., Edwards, Bob, and Diani, Mario. 2001. "Social Capital Reconsidered," in B. Edwards, M. W. Foley, and M. Diani (eds), *Beyond Tocqueville: Civil Society and the Social Capital Debate in Comparative Perspective*. Hanover, NH: University Press of New England, pp. 266–80.

Foster, Kirk A. and Maas, Carl D. 2016. "An Exploratory Factor Analysis of the Resource Generator-United States: A Social Capital Measure" *British Journal of Social Work* 46: 8–26.

Fujiwara, Takeo and Kawachi, Ichiro. 2008a. "Social Capital and Health: A Study of Adult Twins in the US." *American Journal of Preventive Medicine* 35: 139–44.

Fujiwara, Takeo and Kawachi, Ichiro. 2008b. "A Prospective Study of Individual-level Social Capital and Major Depression in the United States." *Journal of Epidemiology & Community Health* 62: 627–33.

Fukuyama, Francis. 1995a. *Trust: The Social Virtues and the Creation of Prosperity*. New York: Free Press.

Fukuyama, Francis. 1995b. "Social Capital and the Global Economy." *Foreign Affairs* 74: 89–103.

Fukuyama, Francis. 2001. "Social Capital, Civil Society and Development." *Third World Quarterly* 22: 7–20.

Fukuyama, Francis. 2002. "Social Capital and Development: The Coming Agenda." *SAIS Review* 22: 23–37.

Gil de Zúñiga, Homero, Bachmann, Ingrid, Hsu, Shih-Hsien, and Brundidge, Jennifer. 2013. "Expressive Versus Consumptive Blog Use: Implications for Interpersonal Discussion and Political Participation." *International Journal of Communication* 7: 1538–59.

Gil de Zúñiga, Homero, Barnidge, Matthew, and Scherman, Andrés. 2017. "Social Media Social Capital, Offline Social Capital, and Citizenship: Exploring Asymmetrical Social Capital Effects." *Political Communication* 34: 44–68.

Gil de Zúñiga, Homero, Jung, Nakwon, and Valenzuela, Sebastian. 2012. "Social Media Use for News and Individuals' Social Capital, Civic Engagement and Political Participation." *Journal of Computer-Mediated Communication* 17: 319–36.

Ginwright, Shawn A. 2007. "Black Youth Activism and the Role of Critical Social Capital in Black Community Organizations." *American Behavioral Scientist* 51: 403–18.

Giordano, Giuseppe N. and Lindström, Martin. 2011. "Social Capital and Change in Psychological Health over Time." *Social Science & Medicine* 72: 1219–29.

Giordano, Giuseppe N. and Lindström, Martin. 2016. "Trust and Health: Testing the Reverse Causality Hypothesis." *Journal of Epidemiology and Community and Health* 70: 10–16.

Giordano, Giuseppe N., Björk, Jonas, and Lindström, Martin. 2012. "Social Capital and Self-rated Health – A Study of Temporal (Causal) Relationship." *Social Science & Medicine* 75: 340–8.

Glanville, Jennifer L. 2004. "Voluntary Associations and Social Network Structure: Why Organizational Location and Type Are Important." *Sociological Forum* 19: 465–91.

Glanville, Jennifer L. and Bienenstock, Elisa J. 2009. "A Typology for Understanding the Connections among the Different Forms of Social Capital." *American Behavioral Scientist* 52: 1507–30.

Glanville, Jennifer L. and Story, William T. 2018. "Social Capital and Self-rated Health: Clarifying the Role of Trust." *Social Science Research* 71: 98–108.

Granovetter, Mark S. 1973. "The Strength of Weak Ties." *American Journal of Sociology* 78: 1360–80.

Granovetter, Mark S. 1974. *Getting a Job: A Study of Contacts and Careers.* Chicago: University of Chicago Press.

Granovetter, Mark S. 1985. "Economic Action and Social Structure: The Problem of Embeddedness." *American Journal of Sociology* 91: 481–510.

Griep, Rosane Härter, Santos, Simone M., de Oliveira, Letícia, da Fonseca, Maria de Jesus Mendes, Guimarães de Mello Alves, Márcia, Souto, Ester Paiva, et al. 2013. "Social Capital in ELSA-Brasil: Test-retest Reliability of the Resource Generator Scale." *Revista de Saúde Pública* 47: 131–9.

Grodecki, Mateusz. 2019. "Building Social Capital: Polish Football Supporters through the Lens of James Coleman's Conception." *International Review for the Sociology of Sport* 54: 459–78.

Halpern, David. 2005. *Social Capital.* Cambridge: Polity Press.

Hamano, Tsuyoshi, Fujisawa, Yoshikazu, Ishida, Yu, Subramanian, Sankaran V., and Kawachi, Ichiro. 2010. "Social Capital and Mental Health in Japan: A Multilevel Analysis." *PLoS ONE* 5. DOI: 10.1371/journal.pone.0013214.

Han, Sehee. 2013. "Compositional and Contextual Associations of Social Capital and Self-rated Health in Seoul, South Korea: A Multilevel Analysis of Longitudinal Evidence." *Social Science & Medicine* 80: 113–20.

Handy, Femida, Cnaan, Ram A., Hustinx, Lesley, Kang, Chulhee, et al. 2010. "A Cross-Cultural Examination of Student Volunteering: Is it All about Resume Building?" *Nonprofit and Voluntary Sector Quarterly* 39: 498–523.

Hardin, Russell. 1993. "The Street-Level Epistemology of Trust." *Politics & Society* 21: 505–29.

Hardin, Russell. 2002. *Trust and Trustworthiness.* New York: Russell Sage Foundation.

Hardin, Russell. 2006. *Trust.* Cambridge: Polity.

Harpham, Trudy. 2008. "The Measurement of Community Social Capital through Surveys," in I. Kawachi, S. V. Subramanian, and

D. Kim (eds), *Social Capital and Health*. New York: Springer, pp. 51–62.

Haveman, Robert and Smeeding, Timothy. 2006. "The Role of Higher Education in Social Mobility." *The Future of Children* 16: 125–50.

Hawe, Penelope and Shiell, Alan. 2000. "Social Capital and Health Promotion: A Review." *Social Science & Medicine* 51: 871–85.

Helliwell, John F., Huang, Haifang, and Wang, Shun. 2014. "Social Capital and Well-being in Times of Crisis." *Journal of Happiness Studies* 15: 145–62.

Hensel, Kyle and Deis, Michael H. 2010. "Using Social Media to Increase Advertising and Improve Marketing." *The Entrepreneurial Executive* 15: 87–98.

Hofer, Matthias and Aubert, Viviane. 2013. "Perceived Bridging and Bonding Social Capital on Twitter: Differentiating between Followers and Followees." *Computers in Human Behavior* 29: 2134–42.

Homans, George C. 1951. *The Human Group*. London: Routledge & Kegan Paul.

Homans, George C. 1958. "Social Behavior as Exchange." *American Journal of Sociology* 63: 597–606.

Hoogerbrugge, Marloes M. and Burger, Martijn J. 2018. "Neighborhood-Based Social Capital and Life Satisfaction: The Case of Rotterdam, the Netherlands." *Urban Geography* 39: 1484–1509.

Huang, Xianbi. 2008. "Guanxi Networks and Job Searches in China's Emerging Labor Market: a Qualitative Investigation". *Work, Employment and Society* 22: 467–84.

Ikeda, Ken'ichi and Richey, Sean E. 2005. "Japanese Network Capital: The Impact of Social Networks on Japanese Political Participation." *Political Behavior* 27: 239–60.

Ingen, Erik van and Kalmijn, Matthijs. 2010. "Does Voluntary Association Participation Boost Social Resources?" *Social Science Quarterly* 91: 493–510.

Isham, Jonathan, Kolodinsky, Jane, and Kimberly, Garrett. 2006. "The Effects of Volunteering for Nonprofit Organizations on Social Capital Formation." *Nonprofit and Voluntary Sector Quarterly* 35: 367–83.

Iwase, Toshihide, Suzuki, Etsuji, Fujiwara, Takeo, Takao, Soshi, Doi, Hiroyuki, and Kawachi, Ichiro. 2012. "Do Bonding and Bridging Social Capital have Differential Effects on Self-rated Health? A Community-based Study in Japan." *Journal of Epidemiology and Community Health* 66: 557–62.

Jencks, Christopher, Crouse, James, and Mueser, Peter. 1983. "The Wisconsin Model of Status Attainment: A National Replication with Improved Measures of Ability and Aspiration." *Sociology of Education* 56: 3–19.

Katz, Elihu and Lazarsfeld, Paul F. 1955. *Personal Influence: The Part Played by People in the Flow of Mass Communications*. New York: Free Press.

Kawachi, Ichiro. 2006. "Commentary: Social Capital and Health: Making the Connections One Step at the Time." *International Journal of Epidemiology* 35: 989–93.

Kawachi, Ichiro, Kennedy, Bruce P., and Glass, Roberta. 1999. "Social Capital and Self-rated Health: A Contextual Analysis." *American Journal of Public Health* 89: 1187–93.

Kawachi, Ichiro, Kennedy, Bruce P., Lochner, Kimberly, and Prothrow-Stith, Deborah. 1997. "Social Capital, Income Inequality, and Mortality." *American Journal of Public Health* 87: 1491–8.

Kawachi, Ichiro, Kim, Daniel, Coutts, Adam, and Subramanian, Sankaran V. 2004. "Commentary: Reconciling the Three Accounts of Social Capital." *International Journal of Epidemiology* 33: 682–90

Kawachi, Ichiro, Subramanian, Sankaran V., and Kim, Daniel (eds). 2008. *Social Capital and Health*. New York: Springer.

Kennedy, Bruce P., Kawachi, Ichiro, and Brainerd, Elizabeth. 1998. "The Role of Social Capital in the Russian Mortality Crisis." *World Development* 26: 2029–43.

Kenworthy, Lane. 1997. "Civic Engagement, Social Capital, and Economic Cooperation." *American Behavioral Scientist* 40: 645–56.

Kim, Daniel, Subramanian, Sankaran V., and Kawachi, Ichiro. 2006. "Bonding Versus Bridging Social Capital and their Associations with Self-rated Health: A Multilevel Analysis of 40 US Communities." *Journal of Epidemiology and Community Health* 60: 116–22.

Kim, Seung-Sup, Chang, Yeonseung, Perry, Melissa J., Kawachi, Ichiro, and Subramanian, Sankaran V. 2012 "Association between Interpersonal Trust, Reciprocity, and Depression in South Korea: A Prospective Analysis." *PLoS ONE* 7. DOI: 10.1371/journal.pone.0030602.

Kirtis, A. Kazim and Karahan, Filiz. 2011. "To Be or Not to Be in Social Media Arena as the Most Cost-efficient Marketing Strategy after the Global Recession." *Procedia Social and Behavioral Sciences* 24: 260–8.

Kittilson, Miki C. and Dalton, Russell J. 2011. "Virtual Civil

Society: The New Frontier of Social Capital?" *Political Behavior* 33: 625–44.

Kleinhans, Reinout, Priemus, Hugo, and Engbersen, Godfried. 2007. "Understanding Social Capital in Recently Restructured Urban Neighborhoods: Two Case Studies in Rotterdam." *Urban Studies* 44: 1069–91.

Klesner, Joseph, L. 2007. "Social Capital and Political Participation in Latin America: Evidence from Argentina, Chile, Mexico, and Peru." *Latin American Research Review* 42: 1–32.

Kmec, Julie and Trimble, Lindsey. 2009. "Does It Pay to Have a Network Contact? Social Network Ties, Workplace Racial Context, and Pay Outcomes." *Social Science Research* 38: 266–78.

Knack, Stephen. 2003. "Groups, Growth and Trust: Cross-Country Evidence on the Olson and Putnam Hypotheses." *Public Choice* 117: 341–55.

Knack, Stephen and Keefer, Philip. 1997. "Does Social Capital Have an Economic Payoff? A Cross-Country Investigation." *The Quarterly Journal of Economics* 112: 1251–88.

Kobayashi, Tetsuro. 2010. "Bridging Social Capital in Online Communities: Heterogeneity and Social Tolerance of Online Game Players in Japan." *Human Communication Research* 36: 546–69.

Kobayashi, Tomoko, Kawachi, Ichiro, Iwase, Toshide, Suzuki, Etsuji, and Takao, Soshi. 2013. "Individual-level Social Capital and Self-rated Health in Japan: An Application of the Resource Generator." *Social Science & Medicine* 85: 32–7.

Krippner, Greta, Granovetter, Mark, Block, Fred, et al. 2004. "Polanyi Symposium: A Conversation on Embeddedness." *Socio-Economic Review* 2: 109–35.

Lake, Ronald L. D. and Huckfeldt, Robert. 1998. "Social Capital, Social Networks, and Political Participation." *Political Psychology* 19: 567–84.

Larsen, Larissa, Harlan, Sharon L., Bolin, Bob, Hackett, Edward J., Hope, Diane, Kirby, Andrew, Nelson, Amy, Rex Tom R., and Wolf, Shaphard. 2004. "Bonding and Bridging: Understanding the Relationship between Social Capital and Civic Action." *Journal of Planning Education and Research* 24: 64–77.

Laumann, Edward O. 1973. *Bonds of Pluralism: The Form and Substance of Urban Social Networks*. New York: Wiley-Interscience.

Leana, Carrie R. and Van Buren, Harry J. 1999. "Organizational Social Capital and Employment Practices." *Academy of Management Review* 24: 538–55.

Lee, Tae Heon, Gerhart, Barry, Weller, Ingo, and Trevor, Charlie O. 2008. "Understanding Voluntary Turnover: Path-specific Job Satisfaction Effects and the Importance of Unsolicited Job Offers." *Academy of Management Journal* 51: 651–71.

Legh-Jones, Hannah and Moore, Spencer. 2012. "Network Social Capital, Social Participation, and Physical Inactivity in an Urban Adult Population." *Social Science & Medicine* 74: 1362–7.

Letki, Natalia. 2009. "Explaining Political Participation in East-Central Europe: Social Capital, Democracy and the Communist Past." *Political Research Quarterly* 57: 665–79.

Li, Yaojun. 2015. "Social Capital in Sociological Research: Conceptual Rigor and Empirical Application," in *Handbook of Research Methods and Applications in Social Capital*. Cheltenham: Edward Elgar, pp. 1–20.

Lin, Nan. 1999a. "Social Networks and Status Attainment." *Annual Review of Sociology* 25: 467–87.

Lin, Nan. 1999b. "Building a Network Theory of Social Capital." *Connections* 22: 28–51.

Lin, Nan. 2001. *Social Capital: A Theory of Social Structure and Action*. Cambridge: Cambridge University Press.

Lin, Nan and Ao, Dan. 2008. "The Invisible Hand of Social Capital: An Exploratory Study 1," in N. Lin and B. Erickson (eds), *Social Capital: An International Research Program*. New York: Oxford University Press, pp. 107–32.

Lin, Nan, and Dumin, Mary. 1986. "Access to Occupations through Social Ties." *Social Networks* 8: 365–85.

Lin, Nan, Ensel, Walter M., and Vaughn, John C. 1981. "Social Resources and Strength of Ties: Structural Factors in Occupational Status Attainment." *American Sociological Review* 46: 393–405.

Lin, Nan, Fu, Yang-Chi, and Hsung, Ray-May. 2001. "The Position Generator: Measurement Techniques for Investigations of Social Capital," in N. Lin, K. Cook and R. S. Burt (eds), *Social Capital: An International Research Program*. Aldine de Gruyter, pp. 57–81.

Lin, Nan, Lee, Hang-young, and Ao, Dan. 2013. "Contact Status and Finding a Job: Validation and Extension," in N. Lin, Y. C. Fu, and C. J. Chen (eds), *Social Capital and Its Institutional Contingencies: A Study of the United States, China and Taiwan*. New York: Routledge, pp. 21–41.

Lin, Nan, Vaughn, John C., and Ensel, Walter M. 1981. "Social Resources and Occupational Status Attainment." *Social Forces* 59: 1163–81.

Lindström, Martin. 2014. "Does Social Capital Include Trust? Commentary on Carpiano and Fitterer (2014)" *Social Science & Medicine* 116: 235–6.

Lipset, Seymour M. and Bendix, Reinhard. 1959. *Social Mobility in Industrial Society*. Berkeley, CA: University of California Press.

Lomas, Jonathan. 1998. "Social Capital and Health: Implications for Public Health and Epidemiology." *Social Science & Medicine* 47: 1181–8.

Lundmark, Sebastian. 2015. "Gaming Together: When an Imaginary World Affects Generalized Trust." *Journal of Information Technology & Politics* 12: 54–73.

Marsden, Peter V. 1987. "Core Discussion Networks of Americans." *American Sociological Review* 52: 122–31.

Marsden, Peter V. and Hurlbert, Jeanne S. 1988. "Social Resources and Mobility Outcomes: a Replication and Extension." *Social Forces* 66: 1038–59.

Marx, Karl. 1990 (1867). *Capital: A Critique of Political Economy (Volume I)*. New York: Penguin Books.

Matous, Peter and Ozawa, Kazumasa. 2010. "Measuring Social Capital in a Philippine Slum". *Field Methods* 22: 133–53.

Matzat, Uwe and Sadowski, Bert M. 2015. "Access to Specific Social Resources across Different Social Media: Divergent Consequences of the Time Spent with New Contacts." *Information, Communication & Society* 18: 1139–57.

McDonald, Steve. 2011. "What's in the 'Old Boys' Network? Accessing Social Capital in Gendered and Racialized Networks." *Social Networks* 33: 317–30.

McDonald, Steve. 2015. "Network Effects across the Earnings Distribution: Payoffs to Visible and Invisible Job Finding Assistance." *Social Science Research* 49: 299–13.

McDonald, Steve and Day, Jacob C. 2010. "Race, Gender, and the Invisible Hand of Social Capital." *Sociology Compass* 4: 532–43.

McPherson, Miller, Smith-Lovin, Lynn, and Brashears, Matthew E. 2006. "Social Isolation in America: Changes in Core Discussion Networks Over Two Decades." *American Sociological Review* 71: 353–75.

McPherson, Miller, Smith-Lovin, Lynn, and Brashears, Matthew E. 2009. "Reply to Fischer: Models and Marginals: Using Survey Evidence to Study Social Networks." *American Sociological Review* 74: 670–81.

Melo Zurita, Maria de Lourdes, Cook, Brian, Thomsen, Dana C., Munro, Paul G., Smith, Timothy F., and Gallina, John. 2018. "Living with Disasters: Social Capital for Disaster Governance." *Disasters* 42: 571–89.

Merluzzi, Jennifer. 2013. "Social Capital in Asia: Investigating Returns to Brokerage in Collectiveness National Cultures." *Social Science Research* 42: 882–92.

Mohnen, Sigrid M., Völker, Beate, Flap, Henk, and Groenewegen, Peter P. 2012. "Health-related Behavior as a Mechanism Behind the Relationship between Neighborhood Social Capital and Individual Health – A Multilevel Analysis." *BMC Public Health* 12. DOI: 10.1186/1471-2458-12-116.

Mollenhorst, Gerald, Völker, Beate, and Flap, Henk. 2008. "Social Contexts and Core Discussion Networks: Using a Choice Approach to Study Similarity in Intimate Relationships." *Social Forces* 86: 937–65.

Molyneux, Logan, Vasudevan, Krishnan, and Gil de Zúñiga, Homero. 2015. "Gaming Social Capital: Exploring Civic Value in Multiplayer Video Games." *Journal of Computer Mediated Communication* 20: 381–99.

Moore, Spencer and Kawachi, Ichiro. 2017. "Twenty Years of Social Capital and Health Research: A Glossary." *Journal of Epidemiology & Community Health* 71: 513–17.

Moore, Spencer, Daniel, Mark, Paquet, Catherine, Dubé, Laurette, and Gauvin, Lise. 2009. "Association of Individual Network Social Capital with Abdominal Adiposity, Overweight and Obesity." *Journal of Public Health* 31: 175–83.

Moore, Spencer, Shiell, Alan, Hawe, Penelope, and Haines, Valerie A. 2005. "The Privileging of Communitarian Ideas: Citation Practices and the Translation of Social Capital into Public Health Research." *American Journal of Public Health* 95: 1330–7.

Mouw, Ted. 2003. "Social Capital and Finding a Job: Do Contacts Matter?" *American Sociological Review* 68: 868–98.

Murray, Stephan O., Rankin, Joseph H. and Magill, Dennis W. 1981. "Strong Ties and Job Information." *Sociology of Work and Occupations* 8: 119–36.

Musick, Marc A. and Wilson, John. 2008. *Volunteers: A Social Profile*. Bloomington, IN: Indiana University Press.

Newton, Kenneth. 1997. "Social Capital and Democracy." *American Behavioral Scientist* 40: 575–86.

Newton, Kenneth. 2001. "Trust, Social Capital, Civil Society, and Democracy." *International Political Science Review* 22: 201–14.

Norbutas, Lukas and Corten, Rense. 2018. "Network Structure and Economic Prosperity in Municipalities: A Large-Scale Test of Social Capital Theory Using Social Media Data." *Social Networks* 52: 120–34.

Oh, Hongseok, Kilduff, Martin, and Brass, Daniel J. 1999. "Communal Social Capital, Linking Social Capital, and Economic Outcomes." Paper presented at the annual meeting of the Academy of Management, Chicago.

Olson, Mancur. 1982. *The Rise and Decline of Nations: Economic*

Growth, Stagflation, and Social Rigidities. New Haven, CT: Yale University Press.

Paik, Anthony and Sanchagrin, Kenneth. 2013. "Social Isolation in America: An Artifact." *American Sociological Review* 78: 339–60.

Pang, Hua. 2018. "How does Time Spent on WeChat Bolster Subjective Well-being through Social Integration and Social Capital?" *Telematics and Informatics* 35: 2147–56.

Paxton, Pamela. 1999. "Is Social Capital Declining in the United States? A Multiple Indicator Assessment." *American Journal of Sociology* 105: 88–127.

Paxton, Pamela. 2002. "Social Capital and Democracy: An Interdependent Relationship." *American Sociological Review* 67: 254–77.

Paxton, Pamela. 2007. "Association Memberships and Generalized Trust: A Multilevel Model across 31 Countries." *Social Forces* 86: 47–76.

Peiró-Palomino, Jesús and Tortosa-Ausina, Emili. 2013. "Can Trust Effects on Development Be Generalized? A Response by Quantile." *European Journal of Political Economy* 23: 377–90.

Pena-López, José A. and Sánchez-Santos, José M. 2017. "Individual Social Capital: Accessibility and Mobilization of Resources Embedded in Social Networks." *Social Networks* 49: 1–11.

Petersen, Trond, Saporta, Ishak, and Seidel, Marc-David L. 2000. "Offering a Job: Meritocracy and Social Networks." *American Journal of Sociology* 106: 763–816.

Phua, Joe, Jin, Seunga V., and Kim, Jihoon. 2017. "Uses and Gratifications of Social Networking Sites for Bridging and Bonding Social Capital: A Comparison of Facebook, Twitter, Instagram and Snapchat." *Computers in Human Behavior* 72: 115–22.

Pinho, José Carlos and Soares, Ana Maria. 2015. "Response to Advertising on Online Social Networks: The Role of Social Capital." *International Journal of Consumer Studies* 39: 239–48.

Poortinga, Wouter. 2006a. "Do Health Behaviors Mediate the Association between Social Capital and Health?" *Preventive Medicine* 43: 488–93.

Poortinga, Wouter. 2006b. "Social Capital: An Individual or Collective Resource for Health?" *Social Science & Medicine* 62: 292–302.

Portes, Alejandro. 2000. "The Two Meanings of Social Capital." *Sociological Forum* 15: 1–12.

Portes, Alejandro and Landolt, Patricia. 1996. "The Downside of Social Capital." *American Prospect* 26 (May–June): 18–22.

Portes, Alejandro and Landolt, Patricia. 2000. "Social Capital: Promise and Pitfalls of Its Role in Development." *Journal of Latin American Studies* 32: 529–47.

Putnam, Robert D. 1993. "The Prosperous Community: Social Capital and Public Life." *The American Prospect* 4: 35–42.

Putnam, Robert D. 1994. "Social Capital and Public Affairs." *Bulletin of the American Academy of Arts and Sciences* 47: 5–19.

Putnam, Robert D. 1995. "Tuning In, Tuning Out: The Strange Disappearance of Social Capital in America." *PS: Political Science and Politics* 28: 664–83.

Putnam, Robert D. 1996. "The Strange Disappearance of Civic America." *American Prospect* 24: 34–48.

Putnam, Robert D. 2000. *Bowling Alone: The Collapse and Revival of American Community*. New York: Simon & Schuster.

Putnam, Robert D. 2001. "Social Capital: Measurement and Consequences." *Canadian Journal of Policy Research* 2: 41–51.

Putnam, Robert D. 2002. "Conclusion." in R. D. Putnam (ed.), *Democracies in Flux: The Evolution of Social Capital in Contemporary Society*. Oxford: Oxford University Press, pp. 393–416

Putnam, Robert D. 2007. "E Pluribus Unum: Diversity and Community in the Twenty-first Century (The 2006 Johan Skytte Prize Lecture)." *Scandinavian Political Studies* 30: 137–74.

Putnam, Robert D. and Goss, Kristin A. 2002. "Introduction." in R. D. Putnam (ed.), *Democracies in Flux: The Evolution of Social Capital in Contemporary Society*. Oxford: Oxford University Press, pp. 3–19.

Putnam, Robert D, Leonardi, Robert, and Nanetti, Raffaella Y. 1993. *Making Democracy Work: Civic Traditions in Modern Italy*. Princeton: Princeton University Press.

Reeskens, Tim and Hooghe, Marc. 2008. "Cross-cultural Measurement Equivalence of Generalized Trust: Evidence from the European Social Survey (2002 and 2004)." *Social Indicators Research* 85: 515–32.

Rietschlin, John. 1998. "Voluntary Association Membership and Psychological Distress." *Journal of Health and Social Behavior* 39: 348–55.

Riley, Dylan. 2005. "Civic Associations and Authoritarian Regimes in Interwar Europe: Italy and Spain in Comparative Perspective." *American Sociological Review* 70: 288–310.

Riumallo-Herl, Carlos Javier, Kawachi, Ichiro, and Avendano, Mauricio. 2014. "Social Capital, Mental Health and Biomarkers in Chile: Assessing the Effects of Social Capital in a Middle-income Country." *Social Science & Medicine* 105: 47–58.

Rodríguez-Pose, Andrés and von Berlepsch, Viola. 2014. "Social Capital and Individual Happiness in Europe." *Journal of Happiness Studies* 15: 357–86.

Rosenberg, Morris. 1956. "Misanthropy and Political Ideology." *American Sociological Review* 21: 690–5.

Rostila, Mikael. 2011. "The Facets of Social Capital." *Journal for the Theory of Social Behaviour* 41: 308–26.

Royster, Deirdre. 2003. *Race and the Invisible Hand: How White Networks Exclude Black Men from Blue Collar Jobs*. Berkeley, CA: University of California Press.

Ruan, Danching. 1998. "The Content of the General Social Survey Discussion Networks: An Exploration of General Social Survey Discussion Name Generator in a Chinese Context." *Social Networks* 20: 247–64.

Ruiter, Stijn and De Graaf, Nan Dirk. 2009. "Socio-Economic Payoffs of Voluntary Association Involvement: A Dutch Life Course Study." *European Sociological Review* 25: 425–42.

Rupasingha, Anil, Goetz, Stephan J. and Freshwater, David. 2000. "Social Capital and Economic Growth: A County-Level Analysis." *Journal of Agricultural and Applied Economics* 32: 565–75.

Salamon, Lester M. and Anheier, Helmut K. 1998. "Social Origins of Civil Society: Explaining the Nonprofit Sector Cross-Nationally." *Voluntas: International Journal of Voluntary and Nonprofit Organizations* 9: 213–48.

Satyanath, Shanker, Voigtländer, Nico and Voth, Hans-Joachim. 2017. "Bowling for Fascism: Social Capital and the Rise of the Nazi Party." *Journal of Political Economy* 125: 478–526.

Sawada, Yasuyuki. 2014. "Is Trust Really Social Capital? Commentary on Carpiano and Fitterer." *Social Science & Medicine* 116: 237–8.

Schneider, Gerald, Plümper, Thomas, and Baumann, Steffen. 2000. "Bringing Putnam to the European Regions: On the Relevance of Social Capital for Economic Growth." *European Urban and Regional Studies* 7: 307–17.

Schofer, Evan and Fourcade-Gourinchas, Marion. 2001. "The Structural Contexts of Civic Engagement: Voluntary Association Membership in Comparative Perspective." *American Sociological Review* 66: 806–28.

Seibert, Scott E., Kraimer, Maria L., and Linden, Robert C. 2001. "A Social Capital Theory of Career Success." *The Academy of Management Journal* 44: 219–37.

Seidel, Marc-David, Polzer, Jeffrey T., and Stewart, Katherine J. 2000. "Friends in High Places: The Effects of Social Networks on

Discrimination in Salary Negotiations." *Administrative Science Quarterly* 45: 1–24.

Seligson, Amber L. 1999. "Civic Association and Democratic Participation in Central America: A Test of the Putnam Thesis." *Comparative Political Studies* 32: 342–62.

Sewell, William H., Haller, Archibald O., and Ohlendorf, George W. 1970. "The Educational and Early Occupational Status Attainment Process: Replication and Revision." *American Sociological Review* 35: 1014–27.

Sewell, William H., Haller, Archibald O., and Portes, Alejandro. 1969. "The Educational and Early Occupational Attainment Process." *American Sociological Review* 34: 82–92.

Shah, Dhavan V., Kwak, Nojin, and Holbert, R. Lance. 2001. "'Connecting' and 'Disconnecting' with Civic Life: Patterns of Internet Use and the Production of Social Capital." *Political Communication* 18: 141–62.

Shen, Jing and Bian, Yianjie. 2018. "The Causal Effect of Social Capital on Income: A New Analytic Strategy." *Social Networks* 54: 82–90.

Sherbourne, Cathy Donald and Stewart, Anita L. 1991. "The MOS Social Support Survey." *Social Science & Medicine* 32: 705–14.

Shpigelman, Carmit–Noa. 2018. "Leveraging Social Capital of Individuals with Intellectual Disabilities through Participation on Facebook." *Journal of Applied Research in Intellectual Disabilities* 31: e79–e91.

Silva, Fabiana. 2018. "The Strength of Whites' Ties: How Employers Reward the Referrals of Black and White Jobseekers." *Social Forces* 97: 741–68.

Simmel, Georg. 1955 (1922). *Conflict and the Web of Group Affiliations*. Trans. K. H. Wolff and R. Bendix. New York: Free Press.

Skoric, Marko M. and Kwan, Grace C. E. 2011. "Platforms for Mediated Sociability and Online social Capital: The Role of Facebook and Massively Multiplayer Online Games." *Asian Journal of Communication* 21: 467–84.

Skoric, Marko M., Ying, Deborah, and Ng, Ying. 2009. "Bowling Online, Not Alone: Online Social Capital and Political Participation in Singapore." *Journal of Computer-Mediated Communication* 14: 414–33.

Small, Mario L. 2017. *Someone to Talk to*. New York: Oxford University Press.

Smith, Sandra. 2000. "Mobilizing Social Resources: Race, Ethnic, and Gender Differences in Social Capital and Persisting Wage Inequalities." *Sociological Quarterly* 41: 509–37.

Smith, Vicki. 2010. "Review Article: Enhancing Employability: Human, Cultural, and Social Capital in an Era of Turbulent Unpredictability." *Human Relations* 63: 279–303.

Snelgrove, John W., Pikhart, Hynek, and Stafford, Mai. 2009. "A Multilevel Analysis of Social Capital and Self-rated Health: Evidence from the British Household Panel Survey." *Social Science & Medicine* 68: 1993–2001.

Son, Joonmo. 2013. *Social Capital and Institutional Constraints: A Comparative Analysis of China, Taiwan, and the US.* New York: Routledge.

Son, Joonmo and Feng, Qiushi. 2019. "In Social Capital We Trust?" *Social Indicators Research* 144: 167–89.

Son, Joonmo and Lin, Nan. 2008. "Social Capital and Civic Action: A Network-Based Approach." *Social Science Research* 37: 330–49.

Son, Joonmo and Lin, Nan. 2012. "Network Diversity, Contact Diversity, and Status Attainment." *Social Networks* 34: 601–13.

Song, Lijun. 2010. "Social Capital and Psychological Distress." *Journal of Health and Social Behavior* 52: 478–92.

Song, Lijun and Lin, Nan. 2009. "Social Capital and Health Inequality: Evidence from Taiwan." *Journal of Health and Social Behavior* 50: 149–63.

Steinfield, Charles, Ellison, Nicole B., and Lampe, Cliff. 2008. "Social Capital, Self-esteem, and Use of Online Social Network Sites: A Longitudinal Analysis." *Journal of Applied Developmental Psychology* 29: 434–45.

Stolle, Dietlind and Rochon, Thomas R. 1998. "Are All Associations Alike? Member Diversity, Associational Type, and the Creation of Social Capital." *American Behavioral Scientist* 42: 47–65.

Stoloff, Jennifer, Glanville, Jennifer, and Bienenstock, Elisa J. 1999. "Women's Participation in the Labor Force: The Role of Social Networks." *Social Networks* 21: 91–108.

Sturgis, Patrick and Smith, Patten. 2010. "Assessing the Validity of Generalized Trust Questions: What Kind of Trust Are We Measuring?" *International Journal of Public Opinion Research* 22: 74–92.

Subramanian, S. V., Kim, Daniel J., and Kawachi, Ichiro. 2002. "Social Trust and Self-Rated Health in US Communities: A Multilevel Analysis." *Journal of Urban Health: Bulletin of the New York Academy of Medicine* 79: 521–34.

Svendsen, Gunnar L. H. 2006. "Studying Social Capital in situ: A Qualitative Approach." *Theory and Society* 35: 39–70.

Svendsen, Gunnar L. H. and Sørensen, Jens F. L. 2006. "The Socioeconomic Power of Social Capital: A Double Test of

Putnam's Civic Society Argument." *International Journal of Sociology and Social Policy* 26: 411–29.

Svendsen, Gunnar L. H. and Svendsen, Gert T. 2004. *The Creation and Destruction of Social Capital: Entrepreneurship, Co-operative Movements, and Institutions.* Cheltenham: UK: Edward Elgar.

Teorell, Jan. 2003. "Linking Social Capital to Political Participation: Voluntary Associations and Networks of Recruitment in Sweden." *Scandinavian Political Studies* 26: 49–66.

Tindall, D. B., Cormier, Jeffrey and Diani, Mario. 2012. "Network Social Capital as an Outcome of Social Movement Mobilization: Using the Position Generator as an Indicator of Social Network Diversity." *Social Networks* 34: 387–95.

Torpe, Lars and Lolle, Henrik. 2011. "Identifying Social Trust in Cross-Country Analysis: Do We Really Measure the Same?" *Social Indicators Research* 103: 481–500.

Treiman, Donald J. and Yip, Kam-Bor. 1989. "Educational and Occupational Attainment in 21 Countries." in M. L. Kohn (ed.), *Cross-national Research in Sociology.* Newbury Park, CA: Sage Publications, pp. 373–94.

Uslaner, Eric M. 2008. "Trust as a Moral Value." in D. Castiglione, J. W. Van Deth, and G. Wolleb (eds), *The Handbook of Social Capital.* Oxford: Oxford University Press, pp. 101–21.

Uslaner, Eric M. and Conley, Richard S. 2003. "Civic Engagement and Particularized Trust: The Ties that Bind People to their Ethnic Communities." *American Politics Research* 31: 331–60.

Valenzuela, Sebastián, Park, Namsu, and Kee, Kerk F. 2009. "Is There Social Capital in a Social Network Site? Facebook Use and College Students' Life Satisfaction, Trust, and Participation." *Journal of Computer–Mediated Communication* 14: 875–901.

Van Beuningen, Jacqueline and Schmeets, Hans. 2013. "Developing a Social Capital Index for the Netherlands." *Social Indicators Research* 113: 859–86.

Van der Gaag, Martin and Snijders, Tom A. B. 2004. "Proposals for the Measurement of Individual Social Capital," in H. Flap and B. Völker (eds), *Creation and Returns of Social Capital.* New York: Routledge, pp. 199–218.

Van der Gaag, Martin, and Snijders, Tom A. B. 2005. "The Resource Generator: Social Capital Quantification with Concrete Items." *Social Networks* 27: 1–29.

Van der Gaag, Martin, Appelhof, Gert Jan, and Webber, Martin. 2011. "Ambiguities in Responses to the Position Generator." *Sociologia E Politiche Sociali* 15: 113–41.

Van der Meer, Tom W. G. and Grotenhuis, Manfred Te. 2009. "Three Types of Voluntary Associations in Comparative Perspective: The

Importance of Studying Associational Involvement Through a Typology of Associations in 21 European Countries." *Journal of Civil Society* 5: 227–41.

Vedantam, Shankar. 2006. "Social Isolation Growing in US, Study Says." *Washington Post*. June 23, 2006. Retrieved Jan 10, 2018 (http://www.washingtonpost.com/wp-dyn/content/article/2006/06/22/AR2006062201763.html?noredirect=on).

Veenstra, Gerry. 2000. "Social Capital, SES and Health: An Individual-level Analysis." *Social Science & Medicine* 50: 619–29.

Verhaeghe, Pieter-Paul and Tampubolon, Gindo. 2012. "Individual Social Capital, Neighborhood Deprivation, and Self-rated Health in England." *Social Science & Medicine* 75: 349–57.

Verhaeghe, Pieter-Paul, Pattyn, Elise, Bracke, Piet, Verhaeghe, Mieke, and Van de Putte, Bart. 2012. "The Association between Network Social Capital and Self-rated Health: Pouring Old Wine in New Bottles?" *Health & Place* 18: 358–65.

Villalonga-Olives, Ester and Kawachi, Ichiro. 2017. "The Dark Side of Social Capital: A Systematic Review of the Negative Effects of Social Capital." *Social Science & Medicine* 194: 105–27.

Völker, Beate and Flap, Henk. 1999. "Getting Ahead in the GDR: Social Capital and Status Attainment under Communism." *Acta Sociologica* 42: 17–34.

Völker, Beate and Flap, Henk. 2001. "Weak Ties as a Liability: The Case of East Germany." *Rationality and Society* 13: 397–428.

Webber, Martin P. and Huxley, Peter J. 2007. "Measuring Access to Social Capital: The Validity and Reliability of the Resource Generator-UK and Its Association with Common Mental Disorder." *Social Science & Medicine* 65: 481–92

Webber, Martin P., Huxley, Peter J., and Harris, Tirril. 2011. "Social Capital and the Course of Depression: Six-month Prospective Cohort Study." *Journal of Affective Disorders* 129: 149–57.

Wegener, Bernd. 1991. "Job Mobility and Social Ties: Social Resources, Prior Job and Status Attainment." *American Sociological Review* 56: 60–71.

Wellman, Barry. 1979. "The Community Question: The Intimate Networks of East Yorkers." *American Journal of Sociology* 84: 1201-1231.

Wellman, Barry. 2012. "Is Dunbar's Number Up?" *British Journal of Psychology* 103: 174–6.

Wellman, Barry, Haase, Anabel Q., Witte, James, and Hampton, Keith. 2001. "Does the Internet Increase, Decrease, or Supplement Social Capital?" *American Behavioral Scientist* 45: 436–55.

Whiteley, Paul F. 2000. "Economic Growth and Social Capital." *Political Studies* 48: 443–66.

Williams, Dmitri. 2006. "On and Off the 'Net: Scales for Social Capital in an Online Era." *Journal of Computer-Mediated Communication* 11: 593–628.

Wilson, John and Musick, Marc A. 1998. "The Contribution of Social Resources to Volunteering." *Social Science Quarterly* 79: 799–814.

Wilson, John and Musick, Marc A. 2003. "Doing Well by Doing Good: Volunteering and Occupational Achievement among American Women." *Sociological Quarterly* 44: 433–50.

Woelfel, Joseph and Haller, Archibald O. 1971. "Significant Others, the Self-Reflexive Act and the Attitude Formation Process." *American Sociological Review* 36: 74–87.

Wollebaek, Dag and Selle, Per. 2002. "Does Participation in Voluntary Associations Contribute to Social Capital? The Impact of Intensity, Scope, and Type." *Nonprofit and Voluntary Sector Quarterly* 31: 32–61.

Woodhouse, Andrew. 2006. "Social Capital and Economic Development in Regional Australia: A Case Study." *Journal of Rural Studies* 22: 83–94.

Woolcock, Michael. 1998. "Social Capital and Economic Development: Toward a Theoretical Synthesis and Policy Framework." *Theory and Society* 27: 151–208.

Woolcock, Michael and Narayan, Deepa. 2000. "Social Capital: Implications for Development Theory, Research, and Policy." *The World Bank Research Observer* 15: 225–49.

Xia, Min. 2011. "Social Capital and Rural Grassroots Governance in China." *Journal of Current Chinese Affairs* 2: 135–63.

Xiao, Zhixing and Tsui, Anne S. 2007. "When Brokers May Not Work: The Cultural Contingency of Social Capital in Chinese High-tech Firms." *Administrative Science Quarterly* 52: 1–31.

Yamagishi, Toshio and Yamagishi, Midori. 1994. "Trust and Commitment in the United States and Japan." *Motivation and Emotion* 18: 129–66.

Yamaoka, Kazue. 2008. "Social Capital and Health and Well-being in East Asia: A Population-based Study." *Social Science & Medicine* 66: 885–99.

Yip, Winnie, Subramanian, Sankaran V., Mitchell, Andrew D., Lee, Dominic T. S., Wang, Jian, and Kawachi, Ichiro. 2007. "Does Social Capital Enhance Health and Well-being? Evidence from Rural China." *Social Science & Medicine* 64: 35–49.

Zhong, Zhi-jin. 2011. "The Effects of Collective MMORPG (Massively Multiplayer Online Role-Playing Games) Play on Gamers' Online and Offline Social Capital." *Computers in Human Behavior* 27: 2353–63.

Zhong, Zhi-jin. 2014. "Civic Engagement among Educated Chinese Youth: The Role of SNS (Social Networking Services), Bonding and Bridging Social Capital." *Computers & Education* 75: 263–73.

Zucker, Lynne G. 1986. "Production of Trust: Institutional Sources of Economic Structure, 1840–1920." *Research in Organizational Behavior* 8: 53–111.

Index

(page numbers in bold type refer to tables and figures)